A Survival Guide for Heretics

A Survival Guide for Heretics

Aaron Van Voorhis

WIPF & STOCK · Eugene, Oregon

A SURVIVAL GUIDE FOR HERETICS

Wipf & Stock
An Imprint of Wipf and Stock Publishers
199 W. 8th Ave., Suite 3
Eugene, OR 97401

www.wipfandstock.com

PAPERBACK ISBN: 978-1-5326-0391-4
HARDCOVER ISBN: 978-1-5326-0393-8
EBOOK ISBN: 978-1-5326-0392-1

Manufactured in the U.S.A.   OCTOBER 18, 2016

This book is dedicated to the heretics of
Central Avenue Church.

Contents

Acknowledgments

FIRST THINGS FIRST, EMILY, you have been so supportive of my career. Even before I was anything, you believed in me. I wouldn't be where I am at today without you. To my parents and siblings, thanks for giving me a good foundation. To my in-laws, the Voglers, I am immensely thankful for your support of my career since it began more than a decade ago.

So many have contributed to my life in ways that are reflected in this project. (Tiffany Morgan, Curtis McConnell, Jonathan Stine, The Gay Christian Network, Lipscomb University, Fuller Seminary). I am especially indebted to my preaching professor at Lipscomb, Dr. John York. You opened my eyes to philosophy and instilled in me a passion for preaching, and preaching well. You're still a voice in my head.

This book and the journey it represents would not have been possible without my church, Central Avenue. I really don't know who shaped who more. Your openness, love, and intellectual honesty inspires me constantly. Max and Bob, we have really grown up together in this thing. Thanks for walking through the wilderness with me and helping me build something truly unique.

Anyone who reads this book or even just looks at the bibliography can see what an influence Peter Rollins and John D. Caputo have been on me. This book wouldn't exist without them. Pete, thanks for *The Idolatry of God*, it changed my life. Thanks also for your friendship and mentorship. Jack, thanks for speaking at Central and for introducing me to "the event" and "the unconditional."

Your sensitivity and gracious writing style are exactly what we need at this time. I would also like to thank Tad DeLay for being another great resource and friend. Thanks for being so supportive and for reading my manuscript. Your book, *God is Unconscious,* was really helpful to me and this project. Finally, thanks to Wipf and Stock. Thanks for taking a chance on me, believing in this book, and for believing in my ministry.

Introduction

IN THE 2014 HORROR movie *Oculus*, a family comes into posses-
sion of an ornate antique mirror. They hang it prominently in
their home only to discover that strange inexplicable events begin
occurring. It's soon discovered that the source of the menacing
paranormal activity is coming from the haunted mirror. Thus, they
attempt to get rid of it and destroy it but are unsuccessful because
the ghost stops them. The underlying assumption in this film, as in
almost all horror movies, is that the ghosts live within the physical
structures of our world (i.e., a house, a toy, or a mirror) and cannot exist in our world without them. This is a good metaphor for
what's called radical theology, the movement and theory that this
book rises out of.

Radical theology should not be confused with confessional
theology, which is merely the object that it haunts. Confessional theology is the religious structures of our world. It is what we confess
or participate in when we practice a religion (i.e., the beliefs, creeds,
doctrines, traditions, and sacraments). It is the stuff a religion is
made of. Radical theology is not a new confessional theology, a new
set of beliefs, doctrines, and metaphysics to replace the old one. It
is not a religion. Rather, it is what haunts our religions and confessional theologies and like a ghost it cannot exist without them.

Radical theology is the ghost that keeps us awake at night
with questions and doubts. It is what spooks us and our religious
sensibilities and reminds us that we are immersed in mystery and
unknowing. Unlike a horror film, our goal should not be to exorcise

the ghost or destroy the object it lives in but to make peace with the spirit and discover that it's there to help us grow and see what's truly meaningful about our religions/confessional theologies.

In more technical terms, radical theology is a loosely defined movement or conversation within the church that is grounded in Western postmodern philosophy and its critique of religion. The radical theologians that have most influenced this book and much of my work are Peter Rollins and John D. Caputo; who themselves are influenced by Western philosophers and analysts like: Hegel, Lacan, Derrida, Žižek, Tillich, Nietzsche, and Freud.

Caputo describes radical theology as a shift in thinking that is made up of three smaller shifts. First, is what he calls the "Hermeneutical Turn,"[1] an acknowledgment that we all read the Bible through the unique lens of our worldview. This means that all interpretations are subjective and contingent upon our biases and presuppositions which themselves are derived from of our family of origin, socio-economic status, ethnicity, culture, gender, age, occupation, etc. The second shift is what he calls the "Linguistic Turn,"[2] an understanding that just as nobody speaks "language" but *a* language, so no one practices "religion" but *a* religion. Therefore, one must understand the limitations of their particular language/religion and its inability to encapsulate absolute meaning or truth. The third shift is what he calls the "Revolutionary Turn,"[3] an acknowledgment that everything is in a constant state of flux. Nothing about our systems of belief and tradition are static and unchanging. Perhaps it's not always our confessional theologies themselves that are changing but merely the way we perceive them, but this is change nonetheless. These three turns are a great description of what radical theology is, where it comes from, and how it's a paradigm shift in thinking.

Another way to describe radical theology is that it's a method of deconstruction. It's a method of peeling back the layers of our religion in order to understand its ideological roots. Ultimately,

1. Caputo, *Philosophy and Theology*, 45.
2. Ibid., 46.
3. Ibid., 48.

it's about understanding that our theology, doctrines, beliefs, and practices are not some kind of black magic downloaded from God like software off the Internet, but a language of the soul that we came up with, a poetics that speaks of the ineffable and transcendent aspects of our experience. Radical theology is about deconstructing constructs.

However, it's important to understand that the goal of deconstruction is not destruction but a kind of reparation, a correction in the way that we think about religion and participate in its structures. Radical theology is about getting down to "the event harbored in the name of God"; as Caputo puts it so well.[4] It's about uncovering the religion hidden within our religion and focusing on that. As James says, "Religion that is pure and undefiled before God, the Father, is this: to care for orphans and widows in their distress" (Jas 1:27). Here we see James unknowingly practicing some radical theology by deconstructing religion down to love, empathy, and justice. Jesus does something similar where he says that all of Scripture and theology can be summed up in the simple command to love your neighbor as yourself (Matt 22:37–40). Certainly, James and Jesus were not disavowing their Judaism along with its traditions and beliefs. They still participated within the religious structure of their community. However, they did so in a radical way by recognizing that the structures were symbolic constructs pointing to a deeper religion hidden within their religion.

This is the work of radical theology and here we see that it's not just a feature of contemporary Western philosophy, but an idea grounded in the first-century Jewish reform movement that later became called, Christianity. One of the goals of this book is to show that what makes Christianity so unique and meaningful is its roots as a religion that deconstructs religion itself. Jesus shouldn't be seen so much as the creator of a new religion but as a reformer of his own; one who called people to live according to the spirit of the law rather than the letter of the law. Jesus didn't attempt to do away with the law/first-century Judaism but show how it functioned as a kind of poetics that reveals the true heart and will

4. Caputo, *Weakness of God*, 6.

of God (i.e., love, empathy, compassion, mercy, and justice). This motif of deconstruction and reformation is lived out repeatedly in church history and can be seen perhaps most prominently in the Protestant Reformation.

The Reformation's motif of deconstructing and questioning the church's beliefs and practices is best summed up by twentieth-century philosopher and theologian Paul Tillich, who coined the term, the Protestant principle.[5] The Protestant principle is based on the idea that that which is constructed can be deconstructed. Philosophies, politics, cultures, and religions are all things that we construct and are therefore deconstructable. A great example of this can be seen when Luther and other reformers deconstructed transubstantiation (the church's doctrine on the Lord's Supper that taught that the bread and wine are literally transformed into the body and blood of Jesus by the priest during mass) back to its eleventh-century roots as an Aristotelian idea imported into the church by scholars heavily influenced by Greek philosophy. The reformers did this in order to argue that it was a human construct, rather than from God, and therefore not a vital doctrine to condemn people over.

Unfortunately, the reformers didn't understand the full import of what they were engaging in. Their problem wasn't that they went too far in their reformation but that they didn't go far enough. What they should have done was continue down the road of the Protestant principle, the road of deconstruction, and take it to its inevitable conclusions. But alas, they stopped short and ended up replacing one oppressive and idolatrous religious system, that of the medieval Catholic Church, with their own new oppressive and idolatrous religious systems. They replaced one fundamentalism with another. Nevertheless, they were on the right path and what makes this so compelling is that their practice of deconstruction was intrinsic not just to the Reformation but to Christianity itself. Christianity has always been a religion that is about deconstructing religion in order to uncover what's really meaningful about it.

5. Tillich, *Protestant Era*, 134.

In essence, Christianity isn't just haunted by radical theology but *is* (a) radical theology.

Understanding these matters will come in handy while reading this book. However, the goal of this book is not to defend radical theology itself as a theory or a movement. It's only mentioned a few times in the following pages. Like an operating system on a computer, it's running in the background and is producing what's seen but is not really seen itself. To put it another way, radical theology is used here as a lens to view Christianity, to understand it better and to see what's worth saving. Like any lens, it's not so much what you see but what you see everything through. Ultimately, as a pastor and not an academic, my goal here is to help Christians who have been burned by fundamentalism, reimagine their faith and church communities and see that they can survive—that there are some things worth saving. It's been my experience that radical theology is enormously helpful in accomplishing that. I hope you'll agree.

1

Welcome Heretic

ACCORDING TO RECENT PUBLIC opinion polls, an increasing number of people in the United States are leaving organized religion behind and becoming *nones*, also known as the non-affiliated.[1] A substantial portion of these *nones* are leaving not because they've lost their faith but because they can no longer tolerate the hypocrisy of the church. They feel drained spiritually and emotionally by communities that profess love and yet are insular and bigoted, that claim to value truth and yet are intellectually dishonest. Such irreconcilable messages force them to make a choice between being a hypocrite or a heretic and many are choosing the latter in order to preserve some sense of spiritual vitality. Thus, Rabbi Abraham Heschel's words ring true, "Hypocrisy, rather than heresy is the cause of spiritual decay."[2]

These heretics have escaped the spiritual decay of the church only to find themselves in a very lonely exile. While an increasing number of them are exiting the church, they still hunger for spiritual community in a world offering them very few options to feed that hunger. Their questions and doubts have brought them to a dystopian wasteland, and they are not sure where they are

1. Lipka, "Religious 'nones.'" lines 1-4.
2. Heschel, *God in Search of Man*, 10-11.

1

or where they are going. They feel adrift and on the brink of no longer identifying as Christians and/or leaving the church forever. And yet, ironically, many feel closer to Jesus of Nazareth than ever before because they too have become the pariahs of the religious status quo. They, too, know the feeling of being rejected for the heresy of putting empathy, truth, and humility above confessional theologies and religious traditions. This is the faith of the heretic, my faith, and the kind of faith I want to promote.

And by faith, I don't mean feelings of certainty about God's existence or feelings of certainty regarding any theological truth claim. I am speaking of faith as a way of living rather than believing. This to me is the faith to which Jesus called us—not so much a set of "beliefs," but a certain way of living in the world called the kingdom of God. And so, the goal of this book is not to give the reader apologetical ammunition, arguments with which to defend the existence of God, or the metaphysical claims of theology. The goal here is not to convert heretics back to orthodoxy but rather to convert them more fully to the idea that Christianity is a "heretical orthodoxy"; as Peter Rollins puts it, a religion that deconstructs religion and that places right action above right belief.[3] In this way, my hope is that heretics might (re)discover what's meaningful about their Christianity and this screwed up community we call the church.

The goal here is not just to survive but also to thrive by reimagining what it means to be a Christian and to be the church today. For some, this won't seem like survival at all but certain death, and to be honest, it is a kind of death. This is about the death of the religious God and the death of religion so that a kind of "religionless Christianity"; as Dietrich Bonhoeffer put it, might be resurrected.[4] Not a religion without churches, prayers, sermons, and sacraments necessarily, but one that doesn't over emphasize or idolatrize these things.

To be clear, I am a pastor, not an academic, and my heart is for the church and those of us who feel estranged from it because

3. Rollins, *How not to Speak*, 1-2.
4. Bethge, *Dietrich Bonhoeffer, Letters and Papers*, 282.

of the bigotry, hypocrisy, and intellectual dishonesty that exists within its midst. I believe the church is relevant and has something to offer the world if it can just get out of its own way. My hope is that this book might be a survival guide for the church and for those who have left it or are on the verge of leaving it. This book rises out of my experience as a lifelong Christian and as a pastor who has created a community that embodies the ideas herein. If "the proof is in the pudding," then Central Avenue Church is proof that churches can survive in what has been called the radical theology tradition—a growing postmodern movement in the church that sees questioning and deconstructing one's beliefs as a sacrament/orthodoxy (for a more in-depth definition please refer to the introduction). My hope is that this book might inspire people to join the movement and create similar kinds of communities.

Peck's Model

In the 1980s, Christian psychiatrist Morgan Scott Peck posited a model of spiritual development that he discovered was very common among American Christians. Though the model is by no means universal in its application or as linear as it is laid out, it is quite helpful in understanding the way many people's spiritual journeys unfold, including my own. The model's four stages are:

Stage I: Chaos. This stage is typified by a sense of crisis and that one's life is out of control or very uncertain. This crisis can be both epistemological and existential as the individual feels lost in unknowing and meaninglessness. Anxieties about work, relationships, health, personal goals, etc., can seem overwhelming. A person in Stage I seeks solutions and coping mechanisms for these problems.[5]

Stage II: Fundamentalism. This is the stage where the person in Stage I latches onto a religious belief system that alleviates his or her existential crisis or feelings of chaos. The belief system functions as a coping mechanism as it provides order, answers, security, hope, and power. It also provides a worldview that neatly defines

5. Peck, *The Different Drum*, 187-203.

moral categories and tribal identities. Individuals in this stage often have black and white thinking, an anti-science bias, and little to no tolerance for opposing viewpoints.[6]

Stage III: Skepticism. This is the stage where people begin interrogating their beliefs and acknowledging their doubts. Once held orthodoxies are now open to debate including biblical inerrancy, creationism, and other church doctrines. This stage is marked by an increased respect for science, other religions, and worldviews.[7]

Stage IV: Mysticism. This is the stage where one retains skepticism but begins to perceive the divine and transcendent in all things. God and spirituality seem too grand to be confined to a particular religious tradition or theology. One learns to live in the tension of competing ideas. Tolerance and intellectual honesty are now seen as key components to one's faith. Mystery and unknowing are celebrated. Religious practice is seen as a means to an end (a language of the soul) rather than an end unto itself. Empathy and justice are seen as the highest spiritual and moral ideas rather than right belief. Confessional theologies and doctrines may still be held but are held onto lightly as opposed to the strong grip found in Stage II. Stage IV should not be thought of as a destination but as a continuance of the journey, a way of thinking and living that opens new doors.[8]

So often I think when we hear those terms, *mystic* or *mysticism*, we think of someone who plays with crystals, talks about mother goddess Earth, burns a lot of incense, and follows Phish or the Grateful Dead around. Not that there's anything wrong with those things, but that is not the kind of mysticism Peck or I am talking about. We're also not speaking of mysticism as a new kind of fundamentalism. Stage IV is not a new metaphysics or confessional theology to replace the one lost in Stage II but rather a way of looking at metaphysics and confessional theology as a kind of poetics of the soul, a vocabulary of the ineffable and transcendent aspects of our experience.

6. Ibid.
7. Ibid.
8. Ibid.

Although Peck's model is very linear, the fact is that spiritual growth and development is not. Quite often, we find ourselves stuck in certain stages or in the space between stages. We find ourselves regressing and bouncing around between stages or seemingly occupying two at the same time. Spiritual growth isn't linear, but this model provides a helpful framework to conceptualize the way many of us develop. Stage IV: Mysticism should not be thought of as the end of the journey or the goal per se but as the continuance of the journey or a new path on it. Ultimately, words like *chaos, fundamentalism, skepticism,* and *mysticism* need to be seen as mere symbols for deeper experiences that defy categorization and simplistic definitions.

The kind of spiritual survival I'm speaking about in this book looks like Stage IV. While survival doesn't necessarily mean that one still attends church and calls oneself a Christian (Christianity is so much bigger than that), this book is primarily written to those who still find their Christian identity and church involvement meaningful. For many of us, this is what survival looks like or the kind we're interested in. This is a difficult journey full of many perplexing issues but one that is possible to survive and Peck's model is a good guide and one that helps us understand the journey.

What I find particularly compelling about Peck's model is how it is echoed in the Scriptures themselves, as though the Bible itself is a person who has undergone a similar spiritual journey. In the Old Testament, we find Stages I and II. Genesis chapters 1 through 11 are all about chaos and disorder. Consider the stories of Adam and Eve's sin, Cain killing Abel, Noah and the flood, and the Tower of Babel. The unifying theme of these stories is chaos and disorder in nature, humanity, and civilization. Then in Gen 12, Abraham appears and God makes a covenant with him to organize and establish a nation of people guided by a particular religious worldview. The rest of the Old Testament is about that people, the nation of Israel, and how they understood what it meant to be the people of God. The law and the litany of rules, customs, and traditions that defined it can be seen as a kind of Stage II: Fundamentalism.

The God of this stage, like the God we find in the Old Testament, is often depicted as harsh, capricious, and pedantic.

In the Gospels, Jesus not only reveals a much more loving God but he turns the entire Jewish religious system on its head by questioning the wooden and archaic interpretations of the law. He seeks to embody the spirit of the law rather than the letter of the law. He breaks the Sabbath and purity laws by cavorting with the infirmed, Gentiles, heretics, prostitutes, and other so called sinners. He stands as someone who questions the entire religious, social, and political structure. Jesus and the Gospels represent Stage III: Skepticism, and he actually points the way to Stage IV by saying numerous times that he is sending the Holy Spirit and this will represent a new way of being the people of God.

Upon Jesus' death, the temple curtain separating the Holy of Holies from the outside world is torn in two. This is symbolic of the Spirit of God going out into the world and making sacred the so-called secular. God's Spirit no longer dwells in a temple somewhere or just in one person (e.g., Jesus, a prophet, or a priest) but in all of us who do his will. In Christianity, we are the temple of God, "the body of Christ"; as Paul call us (1 Cor 12:27). In the New Testament, we find the church beginning as a sect or denomination within first-century Judaism. However, the church eventually includes Gentiles and becomes a separate religion entirely from Judaism through a process of deconstructing Judaism. One could say that Christianity is a deconstruction of Judaism that started with circumcision and dietary laws and ended up deconstructing religion itself down to empathy and justice. As James says, "Religion that is pure and undefiled before God, the Father, is this: to care for orphans and widows in their distress" (Jas 1:27).

Thus, empathy and justice is pure and undefiled religion. The once-thought eternal rites of circumcision, kosher dieting, and many other traditions are replaced with a kind of mysticism grounded in the idea that religion is about living in right relationship to others and finding God in the simple act of love itself. In this way, Christianity is a kind of Stage IV: Mysticism.

The Scriptures echo Peck's model because the human spiritual journey is itself an echo of our common psychological and physiological journey from childhood to adulthood. We move from a state of utter dependency and naiveté to greater independence and awareness, from immaturity to maturity. The desire to remain at Stage II is not unlike the desire to remain a child and to avoid all that growing up entails, such as taking responsibility, working, dealing with reality, and wrestling with the complexities of life. In this way, Peck's model is true on both a psychological and spiritual level and thereby is quite useful to us as we attempt to understand our own journeys.

My Journey

Like many, I can relate to Peck's model. I was born into Stage II and did not have a Stage I per se as I was born to parents who can be best described as Charismatic/Pentecostal fundamentalists. They, however, had a strong Stage I experience in San Francisco in the early 1970s. Neither of them were Christian, and they experimented with the occult and various other New Age ideations in a quest to find some sense of meaning and power in what they perceived to be a very chaotic and out-of-control world. They purchased a Bible at an occult bookstore and, after reading it cover-to-cover, the one passage that stood out to them was 1 John 4:1, "Beloved, do not believe every spirit, but test the spirits to see whether they are from God; for many false prophets have gone out into the world."

This text convinced them that there were good spirits and bad spirits and that they were engaging with the wrong spirits in the occult. Ironically, the occult lead them to Christianity. In Pentecostalism they found an outlet for their paranormal interests and the promise that there was no stronger magic than Christianity. Upon converting, they quickly burned all their Ouija boards and occult books. However, their Christianity wasn't far removed from their previous lives. Their new-found faith allowed them to pursue their interests in the paranormal and supernatural under the guise of Pentecostalism and the Charismatic movement. They traded Ouija boards, astrology, and astral projection for the Word of Faith movement, demonology, and eschatology (study of the end times).

This was the Christianity I was raised in. I would define it as hyper Pentecostalism, where the focus was not on the ethical teachings of Christ and being transformed into his character, but on having supernatural experiences. I remember being told by my father that unless a church operates in the gifts of the Holy Spirit (i.e., prophecy, tongues, divine healing, exorcisms, etc.) that church is irrelevant. Signs and wonders were not just supposed to be a part of one's Christianity, we believed these things *were* Christianity and what made our faith valid.

Like all forms of fundamentalism, the church and home I grew up in instilled in me a rigid sense of right and wrong, good and evil, us and them. However, unlike other forms of Christian fundamentalism, I was casting out demons and praying in tongues when I was eight. Our world was a frightening one made up of angels and demons locked in constant battle over our souls and well-being. We were told that everything that took place in our lives (i.e., sickness, health, success, failure) was the work of one or the other. Therefore, the most important thing one could learn was the ability to discern the spirits and how to control them with prayer, faith, and Scripture. Angels and demons were treated like pawns on a great chess board that were under our command. You can imagine how stressful such a worldview would be on children. Panic attacks were not uncommon in my house, but we never understood them as such.

I remember waking up in the middle of the night all the time to the sound of my younger brother in the bunkbed below me, praying in tongues in desperate but hushed tones. He would routinely have panic attacks at night that a demon was attacking him. We were taught that such attacks could be fended off by our tongue language along with the proper use of Scripture. Though I think my younger siblings had it worse than I did, I too had my fair share of "spiritual" panic attacks.

One day at school in the eighth grade, I became convinced that I was no longer saved because I didn't feel sure enough about my salvation. Such a thought was perfectly logical if you are told all the time that only those who believe enough and believe the right things are going to heaven. I remember at lunch time looking at the doors of the cafeteria that led outside and contemplating running home to get help from dad. I decided not to and found the courage to make it to the end of the day. Upon arriving at home and finding my parents, I could barely speak, I was crying so hard. They assured me I was still saved and I felt better, but panic attacks like this were common in my childhood and early adolescent years. I must have responded to hundreds of altar calls and prayed the prayer of salvation countless times before I was twenty. I lived in constant fear of sin, devils, and certainly God and his wrath. And yet, I was told such fear was a sign of faith and righteousness.

I was also told that going to doctors and using medicine was an act of unbelief. We believed that faith was all one needed to be healed of anything. We still went to doctors and used medicine on occasion if the problem was severe enough but never without some guilt. The only exception was the dentist, which we went to regularly without even batting an eye. I always thought it was strange that going to a medical doctor was a sign of unbelief but not going to the dentist. The underlying message was to use faith when the problem isn't that severe or that obvious like decaying teeth. This, of course, was a kind of disavowed unbelief, a way of covering up our unbelief with false beliefs, something I will talk more about later.[9] I suppose if we really believed, we wouldn't have had health insurance either, but we did.

Like many others, my three siblings and I were raised to believe that our particular brand of Christianity was the only true and right one. Other Christian denominations may have been saved and destined for heaven but we were the true church because we

---

9. Rollins, *Idolatry of God*, 46.

spoke in tongues and operated in the gifts of the Holy Spirit (e.g., laying on of hands, exorcisms, divine healing, prophecy). All this gave us a strong sense of tribal identity and feelings of certainty and satisfaction. We were like God's special forces. His elite unit who could wage spiritual warfare and change the world with faith and prayer. We derived a certain amount of prestige and power from all this.

Stage II was the story of the first twenty-five years of my life. I cannot remember a time that I was not a Christian. Some of my first memories were that of church. I can remember playing under the pews and sleeping on my mom's lap during service. During my teens and early twenties, I played the drums on the worship team, taught Sunday school, and was a leader in the youth group. Among my church friends, I was known as the guy who brought all his non Christian friends to church and got them saved. All this impressed my pastors, and, thus having demonstrated my authenticity, they even let me preach once in a while.

I was intense and bold about my faith. When I was twenty one, I started a rap-rock/hard core band with my brothers and some church friends. Our purpose was to wake up complacent Christians and start a revival. We played around Chicago in various Christian venues. At the end of performances I would grab a mic and preach a fiery message to the audience of mostly Christian teens. They were typically rants about how they are apathetic and need to start living passionately for Christ. Needless to say, I was a bit self-righteous but the audience usually loved it and it paired well with our angry music style.

It wasn't until I left home for college at twenty five (yes, I was a late bloomer) that I experienced Stage III. I attended Lipscomb University in Nashville, Tennessee, to study theology. Lipscomb is a Church of Christ school and that alone was a big change for me. Most of my peers from my home church went to Oral Roberts University, which was a kind of pilgrimage and right of passage in the Pentecostal world. For me to go to a non-Pentecostal school was seen as suspect and dangerous. I remember when I told my pastors I was going to Lipscomb, they warned me to filter out anything that challenged how I was raised. Always good advice to college students—"Don't accept any view that challenges your own."

My time at Lipscomb was where I learned that there were many ways to read Scripture. I learned that the Genesis creation account was something like ancient Hebrew poetry—itself a profound form of truth—and not a science textbook. Evolution was true and the Bible wasn't as clear or as perfect as I thought it was. I learned about the historical and contingent nature of my beliefs and worldview. I learned about culture and the difference between modernism and post-modernism and how everyone had a worldview that influenced everything they thought. These shifts in thinking weren't as traumatic for me as they were to some. I don't remember any dark nights of the soul where I left a class one day and returned to my dorm room to grieve over my lost faith. Rather, I left those challenging classes feeling liberated from fear and anxiety and like my faith had a greater depth and meaning to it.

Stage III was, for the most part, a joyful and liberating time for me. However, for other Christians I know, Stage III was a horrible time of grief as they lost their faith entirely and no longer wanted to have anything to do with Christianity or religion. But for others, they reached Stage IV, and like me, were able to maintain a Christian faith, although a very different one from that of Stage II.

Stage IV for me has been the result of years of study, conversations with different thinkers, and wrestling with hard questions. I don't know anybody who went from Stage II to IV differently because the truth is, we all have the same questions and struggles. We all feel like many of the answers we were given in the religion of our upbringing are no longer adequate, and never really were. We were just too indoctrinated at the time to see it, but now we do. Now we are too aware of the hypocrisy and intellectual dishonesty that permeates our traditions and we long for something honest and true. And yet, we see so much good about our traditions and don't want to throw the baby out with the bath water.

To be clear, being in Stage IV isn't about over reacting to the emotional trauma one suffered in Stage II. Certainly, many of us in Stage IV harbor some anger about Stage II but that anger can be used in positive ways that brings healing and hope to ourselves and others. This is where I'm at and where many others are also at, even if their story isn't as extreme as mine. I've discovered during my years of ministry that we don't have to have the same stories in order to identify with each other. My guess is that most people reading this book didn't have the kind of experiences I did but that doesn't mean that your experiences didn't leave you with the same feelings of doubt and confusion. If you're reading this book there's a good chance you've had a Stage II experience that was hurtful and you're wondering if there is anything about church and Christianity worth holding onto. So welcome, you're among friends.

Conclusion

In order to communicate the various and complex ideas of this book, I have chosen Peck's model as an outline that will help clarify things. For this reason, the center chapters are titled after his four stages. It makes sense to me that a book about our spiritual journey should read like a journey. This will not only allow readers to relate more to the content, but also to understand it within the structure of their own lives and community.

This is a survival guide, and just like an outdoor survival guide might tell us to not eat this plant, build a shelter this way, or start a fire this way, so a spiritual survival guide should show us the dangers we might encounter in the wilderness and how to best make use of the resources available to us. And to be sure, we are all lost in a kind of wilderness. But the wilderness is our home, and my hope is that we can not only survive, but also thrive out here.

My hope is that this book will take some complex ideas from the fields of philosophy and theology and make them clear and applicable to our lives. Again, I'm a pastor and not an academic, and my desire is to help the church survive and be the body of Christ in the world. Therefore, this book is written to those who are looking for a resource that will help them make that happen.

However, this is not really a how-to guide. This book is ultimately autobiographical by nature and thereby about what has worked for me. Obviously, what works for me might not work for you. While this is always the case with spiritual journeys, there is also much that always crosses over and is relatable.

This book is a distillation of not just my thoughts, but also what I think are the best ideas from the best thinkers of our time on matters of faith and practice. I have striven to organize everything here in the most concise and clear way possible so that anyone can understand these ideas and implement them. Most of what you will find here I have preached in my sermons. This book is not just theory—it is also real-world practice. As a pastor, I can say that these ideas are the inspiration and life blood for a real community called Central Avenue Church. In the final chapter, I lay out exactly what our services look like and how we embody the ethos of these ideas in our ministry. However, whether you are a minister or not, know that these ideas have meant spiritual survival for real people who otherwise would not be in church or probably still call themselves Christians.

2

Chaos

IT IS HARD TO accept just how chaotic and random the universe truly is. Our own galaxy will collide with our neighboring galaxy Andromeda in approximately four billion years. This event will cause stars and planets to crash into each other, while others will be thrown out into deep space by the gravitational chaos. If Earth survives this event, and it probably will, our own sun will kill us approximately a billion years later when it becomes a red giant and incinerates the Earth. This is not science fiction but science fact and such events transpire every day in our vast universe.

Approximately 99 percent of all the species that have ever existed on Earth are now extinct. Disease, natural disasters, and the evolutionary process of natural selection are mostly responsible. We live in a chaotic universe that brings both life and death. We experience this chaos not just externally in the natural world, but also internally as a kind of existential crisis. It is existential because we are self-aware beings who understand our own finitude and mortality. We all know we are subject to time and chance and could die in the next moment from a variety of things, and there is nothing we can do about it. Suffering and death are unavoidable and inexplicable. This perplexes us at a deep level and makes us ask questions like—why do I exist? Who am I? What's the point in all of this? These unanswerable questions generate a deep sense of lack and anxiety within us that we never completely escape. However, we long for answers and some sense of mastery over life and death. Therefore, we turn to philosophy, theology, science, and psychology for answers and coping mechanisms.

Religion provides a unique set of answers to our existential crises. In short, religion has been used in human history as a kind of cure-all for everything, the ultimate answer to life and existence's ultimate problems. There is nothing that scientists can tell us, no doomsday scenario or horrific fact of natural history, that religion cannot explain away or provide a simple answer to.[1] Why is there suffering and death in the created order? The church usually responds, "Because Adam and Eve sinned and this was the consequence or punishment for their betrayal." This explanation is part of a biblical metanarrative the church has worked out of for centuries. This master story or metanarrative for Scripture goes: God made creation perfect, human sin ruined it, so God had to send Jesus to fix it. This functions like a three-act play that spans the story of Scripture from Genesis to Revelation, and it stands as the guiding paradigm for much of Christian theology over church history.

According to this story, Jesus was God's Plan B for creation because we ruined Plan A. In essence, Jesus came to fix what we broke. Through original sin, humanity corrupted not only itself (spiritually and physically), but also the rest of the created order too with evil, suffering, and death. Therefore, ever since Gen 3, God has been working to return humanity and creation back to Eden; a cosmic redemptive process that can be tracked in Scripture from Adam to Israel to Christ and through the church age. Though the roots of this view are found in the patristic era (AD 100–450), it remains the most popular explanation for why evil exists and what God is doing about it. Consider this excerpt from an article written by Rick Warren,

> The reason there's evil in the world is not because of God, but because God gave us the freedom to choose . . . And all of the suffering and all of the death that we see in the

1. Lacan, *Triumph of Religion*, 63–65.

world today are the result because man has chosen to make wrong choices.[2]

Early church fathers like Augustine first introduced this view to us in the doctrine of original sin. According to Augustine, Adam's sin damaged our perfect nature, spirit, body, and soul. We inherited his corrupt nature as a consequence/punishment for his sin because we existed in Adam as seed. Therefore, when he sinned and fell from grace, so did we.[3] This means not only do we have a propensity to sin (the sin nature), but also that we carry the very guilt of Adam. This event and its effects became known as the fall, a term (which may surprise some) found nowhere in Scripture.

Augustine's doctrine also claimed that human sin is the cause of our biological death.[4] Therefore, his doctrine is not just about the spiritual effects of human sin, but also the physical, albeit the physical effects are limited to humanity for Augustine and not the rest of creation. In this way, Jesus came to repair our nature, cleanse us from original sin, and remove the judgment of condemnation that God put on our body and soul. While Augustine and the early church fathers laid the foundation for the contemporary view of the fall, others stood on their shoulders and developed it into the view we see today.

In the sixteenth century, reformers such as John Calvin took the doctrine of original sin one step further and claimed that Adam's sin corrupted more than humanity's spirit and body, but also the rest of creation in unspecified physical ways.[5] One is left to conclude that Calvin was at least hinting at the idea that human sin corrupted the entire created order with suffering and death. It wasn't until recently that many theologians such as Abraham Kuyper taught that sin corrupted nature itself and that Christ was

---

2. Warren, "10 spiritual questions," para. 3.

3. Augustine, *Answer to the Pelagians,* 525.

4. Augustine, *Literal Meaning,* 94.

5. Calvin, *Institutes,* 225.

sent to reset everything back to an Eden-like state.[6] Many other influential modern Christian thinkers solidified and popularized this doctrine of the fall into the contemporary Christian worldview and biblical metanarrative (God made creation perfect, human sin ruined it, so God had to send Jesus to fix it). However, while originating from some of the best minds in church history, I believe these views are based on a misreading of Scripture, and, in any event, conflict directly with known scientific facts about natural history.

The fossil record clearly shows that millions of years before humans existed, suffering and death did. Long before us asteroids were striking the Earth, causing mass extinctions. Predation and disease have existed for as long as living things have. When modern humans came on the scene, approximately 200,000 years ago, we too were in a vicious struggle for survival against nature and each other.[7] Humanity has never existed in some kind of pre-fallen, utopian world devoid of violence, suffering, and death. Therefore, humanity is not to blame for why these things exist. Interestingly, an informed reading of Gen 3, the text at the center of this issue, supports this.

Sin and Nakedness

To understand the Gen 3 narrative, we must first understand its key metaphor or symbol—nakedness—and what it symbolizes within the ancient Hebrew tradition. To be without clothing in the ancient world represented poverty, just like it does now. However, there is a deeper spiritual significance to this motif in the

6. Kuyper, *Lectures on Calvinism*, 73.

7. This is not a study or defense of Darwinian evolution. Questions about prebiotic cell formation and transmutation between species leave much room for discussion. However, millions of years of natural selection and biological evolution within species is incontrovertible. No matter what one thinks of Darwinian evolution, we must concede that the fossil record undeniably reveals that millions of years before humans existed, suffering and death did and that is the real point here.

Hebrew tradition. Throughout the Old Testament, sin is portrayed as something that strips us bare and reveals our true nature. In this sense, one's sin is represented in nakedness and the shame that is always associated with it. Consider what God said to the sinful Babylonians, "Your nakedness shall be uncovered, and your shame shall be seen" (Isa 47:3). And consider what God said to Nineveh about their sin, "I am against you, says the Lord of hosts, and will lift up your skirts over your face; and I will let nations look on your nakedness and kingdoms on your shame" (Nah 3:5).

In an ancient Hebrew mindset, sin and nakedness have this interchangeable relationship. One thing has a way of revealing the other, with shame always being the common denominator. Your nakedness reveals your sin, and your sin reveals your nakedness. In Exodus, we find an instruction given to priests not to create an altar with steps, "You shall not go up by steps to my altar, so that your nakedness may not be exposed on it" (Exod 20:26).

This prohibition was made so that in the act of ascending or descending steps, the priest's genitals would not be exposed to the altar. Exposing one's genitals to the altar was a way of defiling the altar. To subject something as holy as the altar with something that was ritually impure was certainly a sin. Interestingly, similar purity rules have been practiced in Orthodox Judaism since antiquity.

Even today, Orthodox Jews are not permitted to read the Torah or pray naked even in private because nudity is seen as an unclean condition in which to stand before God.[8] Like the altar in the Exodus passage, the Torah is holy. Therefore, to stand before it naked is a way of defiling it with one's impurity. Context is king here. Truly, we all stand naked before God, and God does not blush at our anatomy. He certainly made us this way. The human body is beautiful, but the theological context of nakedness in the Hebrew tradition is what must be understood here. The prohibition of Exod 20:26 makes sense when we remember that Adam and Eve hid from God behind trees after realizing that they were naked (Gen 3:10). To stand before God naked,

8. Satlow, "Jewish Constructions," 431–432.

whether that means standing before an altar, the Torah, or God himself, is a way of not respecting God's holiness. Here we see how nakedness represented in the ancient Hebrew tradition poverty, lack, sin, and shame. Understanding this context is key to understanding Gen 3 and how it's not about a fall from grace but a great awakening.

Genesis 3

The last verse of Gen 2 says, "And the man and his wife were both naked, and were not ashamed" (Gen 2:25). This sentence sets the stage for the entire next chapter and for that reason it's imperative to understand. The only reason the text would say they "were not ashamed" was if there were a reason they might have been. The author is forcing the readers to ask themselves—why were they not ashamed of their nakedness? This question would have been on the mind of the ancient Hebrew reader because of the traditional Jewish aversion to nakedness. Yet the answer to why Adam and Eve felt no shame was simply because they did not know they were naked yet. The moment they ate the forbidden fruit is when Adam and Eve first realized that they had been created naked, and when they realized this fact, they became immediately ashamed of it.

> . . . When you eat of it your eyes will be opened, and you will be like God, knowing good and evil . . . Then the eyes of both were opened, and they knew that they were naked; and they sewed fig leaves together and made loincloths for themselves (Gen 3:5, 7).

Discovering the truth of their created conditions emotionally devastated Adam and Eve. The serpent said the fruit would open their eyes to what was good and evil, and that is exactly what happened (Gen 3:5–7). Even God confirmed the truth of what the serpent told Eve about the power of the fruit by saying, "See, the man has become like one of us, knowing good and evil" (Gen 3:22). Such a statement from God implies that Adam and

Eve's moral judgment of their nakedness was correct. It's not to say that God made them evil as we understand evil, but earthy, finite, and lacking.

The next thing we see Adam and Eve doing after discovering their nakedness was what all sinful humans do. In their shame, they tried to cover up the evidence.

> And they sewed fig leaves together and made loincloths
> for themselves . . . and the man and his wife hid them-
> selves from the Lord God among the trees of the garden
> . . . (Gen 3:7–8).

However, Adam and Eve could not hide for long because God appeared in the Garden and asked three very telling and important questions. First God asked, "Where are you?" (Gen 3:9). The author did not have God asking this question because he wanted us to think that God is incapable of finding us if we are hiding behind trees. The author has God asking this question to highlight Adam and Eve's reason for hiding, to which Adam explained, "I was afraid, because I was naked; and I hid myself" (Gen 3:10).

Adam's response focuses the reader's attention on the fact that Adam and Eve were ashamed of their created conditions, but also that they did not want God to see their sin. They knew their nakedness represented lack and imperfection. Again, the connection in the narrative between sin and nakedness is revealed. Adam's response prompted God to then ask an incredible question, "Who told you that you were naked?" (Gen 3:11). The audacity of God's question here is remarkable because God was actually asking, "How did you discover the true nature of your created condition?" What could be wrong with that? What could be wrong with knowing the truth about the way God made us? The fact is, God is the one who made them naked but did not reveal this shameful truth to them himself. Rather, God let them discover it on their own by doing the one thing he told them not to do; eat the forbidden fruit.

Furthermore, God's question ("Who told you that you were naked?") implies that God had no intention to defend how he made them. Remember, God is asking this question in response to Adam's statement, "I was afraid because I was naked so I hid." God could have said, "Why hide? There is nothing wrong with the way I made you. There is no shame in being naked. Take those coverings off. You're perfect just as I made you." Yet God's question here actually reinforces the shame that Adam and Eve have for their nakedness because all God wants to know is who to blame for them finding out! Therefore, God's question cannot imply that he thought their nakedness was good (*good* in the sense of holiness, purity, or completeness). This is further reinforced when God clothes them with animal hides to cover their nakedness more effectively than with leaves (Gen 3:21).

The punishment from God to Adam and Eve (i.e., mortality, hard work for Adam, and increased pain in childbirth for Eve) was a direct result of their eyes being opened to reality. This was not literal punishment for a literal crime but part of the allegory for humanity's new realization that life on Earth isn't paradise but is harsh and unfair. Along with realizing their own sinfulness, they realized that physical suffering and death is a reality that their entire realm experiences. They have realized that they are in a strange conflict against nature itself.

> Cursed is the ground because of you; in toil you shall eat of it all the days of your life; thorns and thistles it shall bring forth for you . . . you are dust, and to dust you shall return . . . (Gen 3:17–19).

In the end, God banished Adam and Eve from the Garden, telling them they could never return. Again, this was not literal punishment for a literal crime but was symbolic of humanity's realization that we can never return to innocence. Humanity had just realized that we are moral agents living in an imperfect world. We choose to do wrong despite knowing it is wrong. Evil exists in us and in nature. The simplicity and innocence, which the Garden symbolized, was no longer possible with what humanity now knew about itself.

At the center of this narrative, we find two competing wills at work with Adam and Eve caught in the middle. God did not want Adam and Eve to eat the forbidden fruit and the serpent did. It is important to understand that God and the serpent in the allegory are not so much metaphors for a real Satan and God but are metaphors for the conflict within humanity between good and evil. This narrative is not about how God punished all creation for humanity's betrayal of him. This story is about an awakening, a loss of innocence and naiveté regarding the true created condition of ourselves and our world. It is a story about humanity realizing and coming to terms with reality, morality, and mortality. It's a coming-of-age story about the human spiritual genesis and the genesis of our existential crisis where we learned that we are immersed in chaos and lack.

Paul's Take

Paul echoes this reading of Gen 3 where he says, "The sting of death is sin" (1 Cor 15:56). Judging from the surrounding context, Paul is saying that the consequence of being made mortal is to be sinful, lacking, unholy, and prone to doing evil despite knowing it is evil. Paul was making the claim that we're this way because we were made mortal and of the Earth. Notice, Paul does not say the opposite—that the sting of sin is death. Human sin did not cause human mortality; rather, the opposite. While Paul says in Rom 6:23, "The wages of sin is death," here Paul is discussing a spiritual death that occurs as a result of sin, not a physical death like in 1 Cor 15. Defining Paul's redemptive metaphysics or his understanding of spiritual death is an entirely different subject matter and will not be dealt with here. Consider this passage of his as well:

> For since death came through a human being [Adam], the resurrection of the dead has also come through a human being [Jesus] (1 Cor 15:21).

Many read such passages through an Augustinian lens and falsely believe that we inherit Adam's sin nature and mortality as a consequence/punishment for his mistake. But if that's true and we are all unwillingly subjected to it, then why not also the resurrection? Is Paul teaching universalism here? I don't think so. Paul can be better understood as teaching that sin and death are inevitable for all humans because we are all made mortal and sinful. We are all made from the same dust as Adam (Gen 2:7; 1 Cor 15:47). Sin and mortality are both tied inextricably to our "dustiness" (1 Cor 15:56). In this way, we can be said to have inherited Adam and Eve's nature, not as a consequence of their mistake, but because we are of the dust, too.

Conclusion

What I believe we should learn from this reading of Scripture is to embrace the world the way it really is. Unlike many pastors and Christian authors today, the author(s) of Genesis do not make excuses for God or provide us with apologetics for why he would make a world like this one. There are no intellectual gymnastics employed to try and clean up God's image. Rather, they subtly invite us to simply embrace the hard truth of our lives and to live in the world the way it really is. This is a kind of coming of age, as Bonhoeffer put it,

> So our coming of age leads us to a true recognition of our situation before God. God would have us know that we must live as men who manage our lives without him. The God who is with us is the God who forsakes us (Mark 15.34). The God who lets us live in the world without the working hypothesis of God is the God before whom we stand continually. Before God and with God we live without God.[9]

In the Garden we find humanity waking up to the fact that we live before God in a Godless world, a world endowed with chaos,

9. Bethge, *Dietrich Bonhoeffer, Letters and Papers from Prison*, 134.

suffering, and death. The cross takes this motif a step further and shows us a God who is not distant and far removed from our situation but embedded within it as Bonhoeffer says,

> God lets himself be pushed out of the world on to the cross. He is weak and powerless in the world, and that is precisely the way, the only way, in which he is with us and helps us. Matt. 8.17 makes it quite clear that Christ helps us, not by virtue of omnipotence, but by virtue of his weakness and suffering.[10]

The cross offers us a God who is not a working hypothesis or an explanation for the world but the total embrace of the world as it really is in all of its Godless chaos. Christianity therefore is about accepting Christ's invitation to share in his sufferings, to embrace the world as we see in Luke 9:23, "If any want to become my followers, let them deny themselves and take up their cross daily and follow me."

The place we are following Jesus to with our cross is that place where we too will cry out as he did, "My God, my God why have you forsaken me" (Matt 27:46)—that place where we too will acknowledge the absence of God in the world and undergo a kind of death. This is the subversive nature of Christianity. It is the radical embrace of the chaos of our lives and world so that we might experience a resurrection of sorts, which we'll get to later on. However, religion is so often about escaping the truth about our lives and world. What often attracts people to faith and religion are its explanations, how it tries to make sense out of the chaos, and offers us a kind of psychological relief. This is how fundamentalism works and is the subject of the next chapter.

10. Ibid.

3

Fundamentalism

"Fundamentalism isn't the problem, it's a solution to the problem."[1] —Peter Rollins

THE "PROBLEM" PETER ROLLINS speaks of is chaos—the existential crisis we are all immersed in which is defined in the previous chapter. We hunger for that which will alleviate this crisis and provide us with order, certainty, fulfillment, and meaning. Our hunger for these things is so pervasive and powerful that anyone who is selling a product or service is ultimately selling these things. The message behind most commercial advertisements is—buy this/consume that and you'll be happy, fulfilled, and satisfied. The same message is found in most churches—think this/believe that and you'll be happy, fulfilled, and satisfied.[2]

This is fundamentalism, and it can function as a solution to the problem in the same way that drugs and alcohol are solutions to an addict for the problem of unhealed psychological trauma like a messy breakup or an abusive upbringing. The drugs and alcohol are unhealthy coping mechanisms and ways of covering up what

1. Rollins, "Is Fundamentalism a Problem," title.
2. Rollins, *Idolatry of God*, 23.

we're too afraid to face. It is a way of numbing ourselves from the pain of our story. Obviously the addiction is a problem, but it's a solution for the deeper underlying problem that must be dealt with for the addict to get sober. Religion can function this way too and become just as much of an addictive substance. Consider for example the story of the rich young ruler:

> As he was setting out on a journey, a man ran up and knelt before him, and asked him, "Good Teacher, what must I do to inherit eternal life?" Jesus said to him, "Why do you call me good? No one is good but God alone. You know the commandments: 'You shall not murder; You shall not commit adultery; You shall not steal; You shall not bear false witness; You shall not defraud; Honor your father and mother.'" He said to him, "Teacher, I have kept all these since my youth." Jesus, looking at him, loved him and said, "You lack one thing; go, sell what you own, and give the money* to the poor, and you will have treasure in heaven; then come, follow me." When he heard this, he was shocked and went away grieving, for he had many possessions (Mark 10:17–22).

His commitment to keeping the law was admirable but there was also something deeply unhealthy about it because he believed that his understanding of the law and the prophets was a kind of salvation formula. You can see how his hubris and arrogance allowed him to live in denial about the true condition of his heart, which was full of greed and the worship of wealth and power. The man was not keeping the law and wasn't as righteous as he thought he was. This revelation was devastating to him and was why he left in sorrow. We see in this story something like an intervention taking place where Jesus refused to enable the man's addiction to certainty and self-righteousness. This is such an important lesson because a lot of us, including me, have spent time being the rich young ruler. Or, as we also like to call ourselves, "recovering fundamentalists."

Being in Recovery

The real problem for us is that we're scared and harbor some deep-seated anxieties about the world and our lives. We crave as most people do, some sense of control and power over what is essentially a world that is out of control. Fundamentalism promises certainty and simplicity, power and control. It says—if you believe these twenty things about God, Jesus, the Bible, and the afterlife, you're guaranteed eternal life and a pretty good life now, too. We're told that God has this perfect blueprint of a life already mapped out for us. He knows who we're supposed to marry, what college to attend, what career path to choose, etc. The unsaid promise/lie here is that all these material things will give us satisfaction and fulfillment. But in order to get God's perfect blueprint for our lives and the satisfaction and fulfillment that comes from it, we have to "follow" him (i.e., pray enough, be sensitive to his leading, tithe, be righteous enough, believe enough, etc.). This of course is found nowhere in Scripture and is a product of the American dream mixed with Evangelical theology. As someone who grew up in this worldview, I can testify as to how oppressive it is and how it creates incredible amounts of stress and anxiety. I spent years wringing my hands wondering if I had missed God's perfect will because I hadn't had enough faith or missed some sign or cue.

Understood at a deeper level, fundamentalism is all about control—controlling God, controlling people, controlling life and death. The fundamentalist believes that if I do A, God must do B in my life, career, relationships, finances, etc. To challenge this idea causes great backlash because it threatens to take away people's source of power and control. This is why so many Christians are afraid of science, doubt, ambiguity, and other religions. They're afraid because those things threaten to take away their power, control, certainty, and satisfaction. It threatens their addiction to that which numbs them to the truth of their lives. Religion has performed this function for a long time. We find a perfect example of this in the Old Testament where Judaism rises out of the chaos of primordial history.

Fundamentalism Then and Now

The first eleven chapters of Genesis are about the chaos of our world and the human condition (falls, fratricides, floods, and failed civilizations). Out of this mess, Abram is introduced in Gen 12 and a covenant is made that will set the stage for a nation and a religion built upon law and ritual. The laws and rituals of Israel function as a kind of rigid fundamentalism. God is depicted like the brutal and capricious tribal gods of Israel's neighbors. YHWH tells Israel to stone everyone from adulterers and homosexuals to disobedient children and Sabbath breakers (Lev 20). He instructs Israel to commit genocide and kill every last man, woman, child, and animal in neighboring nations in order to purify the land (Deut 20:17). Religious and moral laws are to be followed without question and the penalties are severe for noncompliance.

Like any rigid religious system, the beliefs and practices are not just a way of creating and maintaining tribal identity, but are also a kind of catharsis—a way of relieving the community of its internal antagonisms over morality and mortality. The ancient Hebrew tradition of scapegoating is a great example of this. Once a year, the high priest would not only make blood sacrifices to atone for Israel's sins but would take a goat and lay his hands on its head and pronounce over it the sins of the nation. The goat was then taken out of the camp and driven into the wilderness, never to be seen again. The idea is that the same thing happens to their sin—it's driven away into oblivion (Lev 16:20–22). Thus, the goat becomes the embodiment of the people's deepest anxieties. Religious practice and belief has always functioned this way and continues to today within Evangelicalism.

Here we find a kind of diet Judaism or Judaism light. We're told that Christianity is just a simpler set of laws and rituals to abide by, as if Jesus said, "Hey, good news, everybody: I've come so that your salvation is no longer contingent on being circumcised, keeping kosher, performing temple sacrifices, and a host of other really cumbersome laws and rituals. Now you can be saved and go to heaven simply by believing these seven things about my life, death, and resurrection: being water baptized, attending church, and being a good person."

Christianity is not diet Judaism. It's actually a completely new way to think about God and what it means to be God's people. We'll get to that later on, but at this point, it is important to understand how fundamentalism functions within our religion. How, just like ancient Judaism, it gives the practitioner certainty, satisfaction, and power by working a set of rules or formulas. It gives us a sense of mastery over life and the anxieties and antagonisms we all face as human beings. Like a drug, it provides us with an escape from the world and its problems. It allows us to cover up the chaos.

As a pastor of even a very progressive Christian church, I still see this all the time. Some people are drawn to my church out of a sense of desperation. The first Sunday they attend they'll tell me that their life is in shambles as a result of a divorce, financial crisis, or some kind of major loss or loneliness. They feel like God and the church is the only thing they can turn to for help. My heart always goes out to them and I make them feel welcome and pray with them. However, I know that they'll probably only stay for as long as their sense of crisis lasts. As soon as they reach some of kind stable emotional state, they'll stop attending. I've seen it happen time and time again. I even have a name for these folks. I call them shooting stars because they explode into the community and shine very bright for a few moments and then disappear forever.

They attend service every week for a month or two. They come up front every Sunday for prayer and attend every other church function available. Yet, their commitment and passion lasts only as long as their sense of crisis does and then they're gone forever no matter how much I reach out to them with emails and phone calls. My guess is that such folks don't stay very long not just because their sense of acute crisis passes, but also because we don't provide them with the drug of fundamentalism.

They come to us looking for relief, and we offer them love and understanding but that's it. We don't tell them that God's going to make everything okay. There is no snake oil offered, no classes they're told to attend where they're given the spiritual knowledge and power to get control over their lives. In fact, we tell everyone the opposite—that there are no magic formulas or secret powers to tap into that will give them the good life. God won't make everything okay. However, many churches are selling such snake oil (either implicitly or explicitly), and perhaps this is where they go when they leave us. And this raises an important point—fundamentalism is everywhere. However, I think when most people, even fundamentalists, think of fundamentalism they think of some extreme example like the Westboro Baptist Church, or some street-corner preacher ranting about fire and brimstone.

Often fundamentalism is a lot more subtle than that and comes couched in a veneer of progressivism and tolerance. Even in more progressive churches the idea is often still taught that there is some ultimate theological truth to be had, some set of beliefs and practices that is the true Christianity. Even in such "progressive" churches there exists a subtle xenophobia, an us-verses-them mentality still within their ideology and rhetoric. This phenomenon has been called neo-fundamentalism and there are lots of examples of it today.

My current home of Los Angeles has seen an explosion in the last ten years of neo-fundamentalist hipster churches where the main demographic is mostly millennials with tattoos that drink and swear, but the core teachings of the church are still very conservative, especially on what's called the three H's: hell, homosexuality, and hermeneutics.

I remember having a private meeting with a pastor from one such neo-fundamentalist church. Like most pastors, he looked like most of his congregation. In this case, he was wearing skinny jeans, lots of body art, and piercings. As the pastor of a growing church in Hollywood, he marveled at how his church was growing despite teaching every week a kind of turn-or-burn message. He said, "Even kids in Hollywood want the real Gospel and not some watered down liberal message about how there is no hell and being gay is okay."

I remember feeling surprised at first but then considered that this is exactly how fundamentalism works. We all want someone to tell us that we have the answers and know the truth and that other people don't. We all want someone to give us certainty and satisfaction, even if it comes wrapped in intolerance and violence. I'm sure he didn't think he was a fundamentalist and I'm sure most of his congregation doesn't think of themselves that way either. Fundamentalism comes in a variety of different forms, but its causes are always the same. It's a solution to the problems of being human and being immersed in suffering, chaos, and lack. Because of this, beliefs can be just coping mechanisms and ways that we hide from ourselves and others.

Theologian and scholar Tad DeLay says, "The expression of a belief tells us something is going on underneath, but if one thing is certain it is that what truly matters is not what gets said."[3] Beliefs are often symbolic of a deeper and unacknowledged psychological crisis in the believer. Thus the old Stalinist saying rings true, "The more you profess your innocence, the more you deserve to be shot."[4] The more one adamantly professes their beliefs, the more you can be sure there are underlying unbeliefs and anxieties at work. For this reason, belief is perhaps the greatest hiding place for unbelief.

Fundamentalism Is a Rejection of Belief

In 1879, a man named Charles Peace was hung in England for murder. He was escorted to the gallows by a prison chaplain who attempted to get Peace to repent on the death-walk by describing

3. DeLay, *God Is Unconscious*, 4.
4. Ibid., xiv.

to him the horrific things that awaited him in hell. The attempt backfired and Peace responded to the chaplain,

> Sir, if I believed what you and the church of God say that you believe, even if England were covered with broken glass from coast to coast, I would walk over it, if need be, on hands and knees and think it worth while living, just to save one soul from an eternal hell like that![5]

Perhaps Peace's background as a convicted murderer and a lifelong criminal equipped him to spot a con job better than most. He saw straight through the chaplain's hypocrisy and unveiled his hidden unbelief. Anyone who claims to believe in a hell for unrepentant sinners or for those with wrong beliefs, and isn't out there day and night trying to save such poor souls at any cost, is either a sociopath or doesn't believe what they think they do. The problem with fundamentalism is that it confuses belief with unbelief and then demonizes anyone who points out the confusion.

We tend to think of belief as ideas and concepts we hold in our heads about God that may or may not have anything to do with the way we live. I once heard about a seminar at a church in Texas titled "Our Beliefs Must Dictate Our Actions." What a strange title. Where else in life do we think like this? Imagine a marriage seminar titled "Our Love for Our Spouse Must Dictate How We Treat Them." The problem with this title is the way it assumes that one can love their spouse and not treat them well. Certainly, marriage takes work and we always have to be learning how to love each other better. But if the underlying assumption is that one can love their spouse and potentially not treat them well, then we've got bigger problems then what any marriage seminar can fix. In the same way, we must understand that no meaningful distinction exists between our beliefs and our actions.

Our beliefs always dictate our actions whether we want them to or not. We don't need to work at bringing them into sync with each other—they already are. And this leads us to a truly helpful realization, albeit perhaps a scary one, that our beliefs

---

5. Ravenhill, *Why Revival Tarries*, 34.

live in our actions rather than in our heads, and if we really want to know what we believe we must simply examine our actions.[6] For example, if I claim to believe in God, the divinity of Jesus, and his resurrection but I pretty much treat people like garbage, then I don't really believe in those things. This is more than just about how faith without works is dead, this is to say that faith is works. There is no meaningful distinction, but we've been taught that there is.

We've been taught that what makes Christianity so unique and great compared to other religions is that it's not about what you do and how perfect you live but about what you believe—which is a fascinating way to think. Since when is believing and thinking not an action or something we do? When we make Christianity about believing the right things instead of doing the right things, we demonstrate that we have no idea what belief is. Our faith lives in our actions, not in our heads, and this means that our so-called beliefs that we hold in our heads can actually function as unbelief, false stories/lies that we tell ourselves about ourselves.[7]

Facebook is a great example of how we do this. Do you ever notice how everybody on Facebook is bright and cheery, and their lives seem like they're going amazing? Except if you know them really well, you probably know that they're not doing nearly as amazing as they seem. Facebook allows us to live in these false stories, to create these idealized versions of ourselves for the world to believe in and for even us to believe in, as well, when in reality our lives are often quite different.

I think we all, to a great degree, live in these false stories that we like to tell about ourselves so that we can avoid having to do the hard and painful work of confronting who we really are and dealing with our issues. And unfortunately, faith and belief can function this way too. Jesus points this out to us himself:

> "Not everyone who says to me, 'Lord, Lord,' will enter the kingdom of heaven, but only one who does the will of my Father in heaven. On that day many will say to me,

6. Rollins, "Courageous Conversations," 23:50–55.
7. Rollins, *Idolatry of God*, 53–54.

33

'Lord, Lord, did we not prophesy in your name, and cast out demons in your name, and do many deeds of power in your name?' Then I will declare to them, 'I never knew you; go away from me, you evildoers'" (Matt 7:21–23).

These people who are calling Jesus, "Lord, Lord," have really good beliefs about him in their heads. They're even out there preaching and performing miracles in his name. But Jesus says they have fooled themselves into thinking they believe in things they don't. If Facebook existed back then, these people's Facebook pages would be littered with pictures of them preaching to crowds, casting out demons, maybe posing with the children in Africa they spent a week with once. But behind the scenes, these people's personal lives, their real lives, look totally different.

To Jesus, one's faith was found in one's obedience to God's will, and Jesus made it quite clear what that was—to love others as ourselves. This was the fulfillment of all the law and the prophets. The emphasis is on love and our relationships with others, not on things we believe in our heads or in religious rituals. This is what real faith and belief looks like to Jesus, and in this way he points out how our belief can actually function as unbelief, how our faith in him can actually be a denial of him, a denial of his death and resurrection. When we think of belief as primarily ideas we hold in our head about God, we are practicing a kind of unbelief and denying Christ and the resurrection.[8]

Fundamentalism isn't so much a way of believing because to truly believe in something, or to have faith, is to acknowledge one's unbelief and doubt. Belief and doubt are like two sides of the same coin. One cannot exist without the other. Belief is not the opposite of doubt but belief actually is a kind of doubt, a way of doubting as if one did not. Belief is not the response to what is known and understood, but it is the response to what is unknown and not understood, that which is unbelievable.

For example, we don't need to have faith in gravity, faith that gravity is going to keep us attached to the Earth; we know it will because we know how gravity works. We know that it is the

8. Rollins, "My Confession," para. 4–5.

warping of space-time around mass. We have empirical evidence for this. We can measure it and test it numerous different ways. There's math for this stuff. Faith in gravity is unnecessary because we know what it is and how it works. Faith is only necessary when reason exists to doubt or disbelieve something. Therefore, to have faith in something like God is to acknowledge your doubt and the fact that it is at least somewhat unbelievable. For this reason, it takes a bit of an atheist to be a Christian.[9] It takes a bit of an atheist to be a believer or a person of faith. To deny that is to deny what faith really is. Faith and doubt are just two sides of the same coin.

Slovenian philosopher Slavoj Žižek said, "A fundamentalist does not believe, he knows it directly."[10] A fundamentalist unknowingly rejects faith and belief in the truest sense of those terms for a counterfeit kind of knowledge, a knowledge they believe is epistemologically identical to empirical knowledge or scientific knowledge.

Epistemology is the study of knowledge itself, the study of how we know what we know, the study of what constitutes knowledge and what does not. The problem for me growing up and for many Christians is that we've been taught that faith and theology is on the same epistemological playing field as things like science, but it is not. Science is predicated, epistemologically speaking, on the five senses/empirical evidence. That which cannot be known empirically and tested according to the scientific method cannot be said to be known at all, which is actually quite true. We really do know that the Earth is billions of years old because of a mountain of empirical evidence in the fields of geology, paleontology, physics, etc. That's real knowledge. We really know that.

Now, don't get me wrong, I'm all for the post-modern idea that there are kinds of knowledge and truth that transcend the five senses, that transcend empirical evidence. How else would we appreciate art? How else would we know what love is and appreciate it like we should? I'm a pastor because I believe there are "truths" and kinds of "knowledge" that transcend the five senses. But the

9. Rollins, "You Don't Need," para. 1.
10. Žižek, How to Read, 116.

35

scare quotes can never come off those kinds of "knowledge" and "truth" because they are epistemologically different from scientific knowledge.

So when we speak about knowing God or knowing things about God and his will for us, we are talking about "knowledge," not knowledge. We are talking about different epistemological standards. And this is because so far God has not allowed himself to be proven to exist, scientifically speaking. Evidence for a creator may exist in things like the presence of information at the molecular level as we see in DNA and RNA. Another piece of compelling evidence may be the fine tuning of the universe's physics, without which life wouldn't be possible. But again, none of this proves God's existence or for that matter comes close to proving the existence of a personal God who hears our prayers, forgives our sins, and grants us eternal life. Science may offer us evidence of a deistic God, an absentee landlord who built everything but is unreachable when the pipes burst. However, one cannot infer from DNA and physics that a personal, theistic God exists who answers prayers and tells us to love each other.

Epistemologically speaking, no theological truths exist that we can actually know. We may believe they are true and they may actually be true, but we do not know they are true. Ultimately they are forms of "knowledge" on this side of eternity. The scare quotes can never come off. This is a hard truth that we must accept, and it carries with it serious implications.

Misunderstanding epistemology leads to intellectual dishonesty and an anti-science bias seen in how fundamentalists can deny that the Earth and universe are billions of years old and believe instead that Gen 1 is the true scientific description of the universe's formation. This is why fundamentalists can believe that their understanding of God and Scripture is the only true and valid one. Such belief in turn leads to xenophobia and even bigotry as those who challenge the "truth" must be stopped or kept out of the community. Such beliefs are really a kind of unbelief and have serious moral implications.

Moral Implications for Fundamentalism

Fundamentalists argue that without religion, objective morality does not exist. They make an epistemological error by claiming that we only know what right and wrong are because God told us (e.g., the Ten Commandments). They say if we don't believe in God, then we cannot believe in objective morality because all we have then are the subjective whims and opinions of mere human beings. For them, saying that murder is wrong is like saying—I like vanilla ice cream more than chocolate. It's entirely based on one's opinion and is therefore entirely subjective. Therefore, they claim we need a higher authority figure than ourselves telling us what's right and wrong; otherwise, we don't have objective morality.

What does it say about us if we need a God to tell us that things like murder, slavery, rape, and stealing are wrong for us to know that they are wrong? A prominent atheist and philosopher Sam Harris puts it well when he says that there are certain ideas and behaviors that we can agree upon as being better for human "well-being" and "human flourishing" than other ideas and behaviors.[11] Rape, stealing, slavery, and murder obviously inhibit human well-being and the well-being of entire societies if they are permitted to go on unchecked. Sexism and racism obviously inhibit human well-being. Physical, sexual, and emotional abuse obviously inhibits human well-being. Corrupt businesses and corrupt governments obviously inhibit human well-being. I think we can say that these things, along with many other things, are morally wrong, bad, or evil because they inhibit human well-being. You don't have to be a believer in God or a theologian to understand this, you just need empathy. This is echoed in a popular but anonymous internet meme:

> You don't need religion to have morals. If you can't determine right from wrong you lack empathy, not religion.

However, fundamentalists counter by saying that theology is the highest moral idea. That wouldn't be a problem if their theology

11. Harris, *Moral Landscape*, 3.

was grounded in Jesus' teaching that the greatest commandment is empathy, to "love your neighbor as yourself" (Mark 12:31). But that is not the theological paradigm such Christians are often working out of. Instead, they are working out of a theological paradigm that can justify unspeakable acts of cruelty and bigotry as long as the Bible says it's God's will. For example, in Leviticus, we find Israel believing that God tells them to stone people to death for an assortment of sins like adultery, homosexuality, witchcraft, and even disobedient children (Lev 20). This was seen as a moral response to all kinds of sins. They also believed that God told them to commit genocide because their neighbors were evil (Deut 20:17). It was also deemed moral and just to beat your slave to the brink of death because they are your human property (Exod 21:20).

Many justify these texts today as mysteries of God's justice that are beyond our understanding. And this must be believed because it's the only way to maintain an inerrant view of Scripture. This reveals the true crux of the issue—you can believe that God is loving and just *or* you can believe the Bible is inerrant, but you can't believe both. And this is something that many Christians are not willing to acknowledge because God and the Bible are seen as really the same thing. Again, this is a kind of idolatry and a way of living in denial of reality so that one can maintain feelings of certainty and satisfaction.

But what really should concern us are the deeper moral and ethical implications. By maintaining a fundamentalist, inerrant view of Scripture, we are saying that genocide, bigotry, and cruelty are not evil if God does it, or commands us to do it for him because God is good and just. In this way, words like goodness and justice become nonsense. They become just hollow moral concepts that can be defined as including even acts of bigotry, cruelty, and genocide. This explains how it's possible for churches to say that it's good and just to exclude women from church leadership and to subject them even in the home with male patriarchy. It's good and just to oppress the LGBT community and to deny them rights in society. It's good and just to support slavery and the entire subjugation of blacks the way many Christians did. It's good and just to discriminate against Muslims and other religions. The list could go on and on.

Fundamentalist eschatology (one's understanding of the end times or age to come) holds some major moral implications too. Growing up in a Pentecostal tradition meant that we took our eschatology very seriously, to say the least. We were obsessed with the end times and seemed to look forward with gleeful anticipation to all it entailed. We believed that wars, diseases, freakish weather, and social upheaval would increase to an unprecedented level and we loved talking about it. While we believed that we would be rescued by the rapture from the worst of it, we reveled in the idea of seeing the world crumble before our eyes. And why not? We believed the world was a fallen and evil place, perverted by original sin and worthy of total destruction.

I remember a Christian comic book I had as a kid called, "A New World Is Coming." It was written by the famous end times expert, Hal Lindsey. In it he shows a picture of the Earth being blown up by God at the end of the age. What does it say about us if we're teaching our children that God is going to destroy the world along with countless lives and that this is something to be excited about? And it is something fundamentalists are excited about. What else are we to conclude when it pervades entertainment media like children's comic books, the Left Behind book series, and films? What else are we to make of this?

DeLay says, "As a theologian, one cannot help but be fascinated by Christianity's desire to annihilate the world."[12] It's fascinating because such a desire is obviously contrary to the Christian values of love and compassion. Schadenfreude has no place within Christianity and yet we find it at the heart of Evangelical eschatology. What are the moral implications of this? How does a desire to see the world destroyed, along with countless lives, inform how we behave socially, politically, economically, and ecologically?

I would argue that such an eschatology creates a kind of escapist and fortress-like mentality. I remember when I was twenty

12. DeLay, *God Is Unconscious*, 5.

three telling my dad that I wanted to travel and see some of the world. His response was, "There's no point in doing that, Jesus is coming back so soon." In other words, there's no point in enjoying life, exploring the world, or having ambitions because we're about to leave this place behind. While my father's views were more extreme than most, one can see a similar kind of logic play out in a lot of churches. The thinking is—why work to make the world a better place? The world is fallen and is going to hell. God is going to destroy it eventually. Let's just wait for the rapture in our churches and Christian subculture where we'll be safe from the world and its corrupting influences. In other words, why rearrange the deck chairs on the Titanic? Care for the environment and social activism is irrelevant if one believes that the world is going to be destroyed soon or that one is escaping via the rapture.

Conclusion

In this chapter we've seen how many aspects of fundamentalism are not just a theological and intellectual problem within the Church, but are a moral and ethical problem, too. This critique applies to all religious fundamentalism—not just Christian but even Jewish, Buddhist, and Muslim fundamentalism. Anytime we have an idolatrous relationship to our beliefs and practices, they can become oppressive for us and others. This can be true for even a very progressive faith, one that claims to value inclusivity and intellectual honesty. Even progressive believers can become fundamentalists and exclude and oppress conservatives. Even progressives can have an idolatrous relationship to their beliefs and practices and think they are above critique or represent some kind of absolute truth. For this reason, I want to make clear that my views could be wrong. I cannot ask others to question their own beliefs and convictions without being open to questioning mine. If I refused to do this, then I would become like the very thing I am critiquing.

A great example of this can be seen in the New Atheist movement where proponents such as Richard Dawkins and Sam Harris attack religion and the religious with a kind of zealotry and intoler-ance that can only be described as a kind of fundamentalism. Thus, they become the very thing they critique. This is what happens when we are motivated more from self-righteousness rather than love. This is how fundamentalism works and why it is everywhere, even in atheism. It's everywhere because we all desire certainty and satisfaction and we are all immersed in chaos and lack.

4

Skepticism

"To believe is human; to doubt, divine."[1] —Peter Rollins

TO BELIEVE IS HUMAN because we all want to believe in something that gives us meaning, certainty, satisfaction, fulfillment, and peace. We all want to be told why our beliefs, practices, and worldviews are right and why others are wrong. However, to question these things is divine because it elevates us out of our drives and anxieties and into the higher realm of self-critique and understanding. Rollins is not telling us to doubt so much as he is trying to get us to acknowledge that we already do. As covered in the previous chapter, we are full of doubts. To claim to believe in something is a tacit admission of doubt because one does not believe in what is proven or obvious. To acknowledge one's doubt and unknowing is the first step in a new direction.

Skepticism is a very fluid stage, unlike fundamentalism and mysticism, which have more defined boundaries. One can be a skeptical fundamentalist and certainly a skeptical mystic, as mysticism and skepticism rely on each other. One is never just

1. Rollins, *Insurrection*, 19.

a skeptic—he or she leans into either fundamentalism or mysticism. Skepticism begins when one begins to acknowledge his or her doubt and unknowing or the hidden cracks within his or her belief system. Quite often encountering different points of view, wrestling with unanswered prayers, or unjust suffering causes this. I entered this stage when I left home and went to college. It was then that I first really engaged in critically examining my faith. I chose Lipscomb because my girlfriend, now wife, Emily, was going to Vanderbilt, which is also in Nashville. My mom questioned my decision, telling me I was "following a skirt." She was right but the best decisions we ever make in life involve relationships and following and/or partnering with the right people. Following a skirt was the best decision I ever made.

There were other schools in Nashville that offered Bible degrees, but I chose Lipscomb because I like the way their program sounded. Even though it was a Church of Christ school, I wanted to try it anyway because I was open to a different perspective than the one I was raised on. This was key, and it is the one thing that is necessary to go from Stage II to Stage III. Simply being curious and having an open mind is all it takes. It makes sense, therefore, why fundamentalist traditions do everything they can to squelch curiosity and open mindedness.

I entered into a crisis of faith at Lipscomb but it wasn't traumatic in an emotional sense. I never had a proper dark night of the soul where I wept over my lost faith and became an atheist like others I know. For some, seminary or even undergraduate Bible programs can be devastating. This is particularly true if one's faith is like a house of cards. In this case even a center-right Bible program can wreak havoc when the card of creationism or inerrancy is removed. Finding out Moses didn't write the Pentateuch or that Paul didn't write Hebrews can be earth shattering. Learning that we have no original manuscripts of the Bible and that what we do have are copies of copies, each with slight or major variations, can be really hard to cope with.

When I learned these things, it wasn't traumatic because I was already confident the Christianity I was raised on was full of flaws. I went to Lipscomb ready to deconstruct my faith and find a new path. I went there assuming I was probably wrong about a lot, and I never really stopped assuming that. For this reason, my crisis of faith has been a slow burn and something I am still experiencing even thirteen years after it started. In a very real way, it's been the theme of my faith journey for the last decade or so. This isn't to say it hasn't been hard. There have been times and still are where I'm not sure what I believe anymore. I feel a sense of loss and fear that nothing about God or the afterlife is real. But this "crisis" has also been life giving and a catalyst for so much positive growth and change.

Skepticism always leads to a crisis of faith. When this happens it's important to understand that we haven't started to doubt, but that we have begun to acknowledge our doubt. We have begun to acknowledge what was there all along but was previously repressed out of anxiety. The crisis of faith occurs when one's beliefs and religious system can no longer hold back the eruption of doubt and questions. As DeLay said:

> The best critiques erupt from within inside an ideology's framework precisely when they can no longer *not* erupt.[2]

They are the best critiques not just because they happen out of necessity, but also because they come from an experienced practitioner with an intimate understanding of the ideological system. Jesus was one such practitioner who performed the role of the skeptic in his ideological system of first-century Judaism. In order to understand Jesus and Christianity, one must understand how it grew out of skepticism, a crisis of faith, and the deconstruction of religion itself as the means by which we approach a relationship with God.

2. DeLay, *God Is Unconscious*, 101.

Jesus as Radical Reformer

Christianity began as a reform movement within first-century Judaism, a religion that had tons of burdensome religious laws and rules. Jesus was branded as a religious heretic and was ultimately killed for it because he violated those religious laws and rules. He broke the Sabbath, broke fasts, cavorted with and touched people who were deemed ritually unclean, etc. The religious leaders killed him because he was seen as a threat to their religious, political, and economic power, which was all intertwined.

In Matt 22:38–40, Jesus essentially reduced the entire Jewish religion to the idea of loving one's neighbor as yourself. This was an incredibly subversive and controversial thing to say, and ironically, it still is. It's ironic because the very religion these words inspired—Christianity—often does not want to bear the full weight of them. It's ironic that it is controversial to be irreligious within Christianity, to point out how religious practices, theologies, and doctrines are always something partial and never an end to themselves but are always a means to an end. This is ironic because Christianity at its very heart is an irreligious and heretical idea that calls religious people to interrogate their beliefs, to deconstruct their beliefs down to what really matters: love and justice.

In this way, the Protestant Reformation of the sixteenth century and the Emergent Church movement of today, along with countless other revolutions and reformations within church history, should not be seen as aberrations but as examples of Christianity doing what it was built to do. This is what Christianity does when it's behaving most Christ-like—it radically deconstructs religion down to what it's all about. Christians who don't understand this are like those people who own tigers or lions as pets and then are shocked when the animal turns on them one day and tries to eat them. Everyone else who hears about it says, "Wow, how did you not expect that? That's what lions are built to do." Just as there is no such thing as a domesticated or tamed lion, there is no such thing as a domesticated or tamed Christianity.

Consider the circumcision controversy in the first-century church. This was a heated debate between Paul and the Jerusalem church leaders over whether Gentile converts had to be circumcised in order to be Christians. It was eventually ruled that they did not, but the controversy nearly split the church in two. The circumcision question has never gone away. It's just changed forms over the years and shown up in the form of other questions like: Can you be a Christian if you're a protestant? Can you be a Christian if you haven't been water baptized? Can you be a Christian if you don't do the Lord's Supper the right way? Can you be a Christian if you're gay? Can you be a Christian if you don't believe the Bible is perfect? Can you be a Christian if you don't believe in the Trinity? Can you be a Christian if you don't believe in the virgin birth or in the bodily resurrection of Jesus? The list is never ending. Thus, Bonhoeffer said:

> The Pauline question of whether circumcision is a condition for justification seems to me in present day terms to be whether religion is a condition for salvation.[3]

There is always a new circumcision question to be asked, always a new controversy about what religious ideas and practices are necessary for salvation or to call oneself a Christian. But such questions always miss the point because they are a subtle rejection of Christianity itself as a conversion to conversion itself, a conversion to the deconstruction of religion itself as the means by which we think of our relationship with God.

I think it helps to understand that Jesus didn't launch a new religion. He never labeled his movement or described it as separate from Judaism. It became known as Christianity years after he was gone. When Jesus gave his disciples the great commission, he didn't say, "Now you're no longer Jews but something else. Figure out a name, build this new religion and make converts to it." No, he said, "Go therefore and make disciples" (Matt 28:19). In other words, "Go and make followers of my teachings and my way of living in

3. Bethge, *Dietrich Bonhoeffer, Letters and Papers from Prison*, 281.

the world." Jesus didn't launch a new religion. He launched a new way of living in the world.

Jesus' teachings and story eventually became the foundation of a new religion, and this isn't a bad thing, we must remember that Christianity is what Bonhoeffer called, a "religionless religion." This doesn't mean that it doesn't have traditions and beliefs but that we should always see these things as means to an end, a kind of language for the soul, and like all language, it is always something partial and lacking, but also necessary and good. Our religious traditions and beliefs are beautiful expressions that cannot be replaced by philosophy, science, and psychology. We would lose so much if we did away with our songs, sacraments, supplications, and sermons. It would be like getting rid of literature or art. These things are unique expressions of our humanity, a kind of language of the soul, but they must be seen in the right light, and I think this is what we see Jesus doing.

A Markan Sandwich

Another great example of Jesus performing the role of a skeptic can be seen in Mark 2:18–28.

> Now John's disciples and the Pharisees were fasting; and people came and said to him, "Why do John's disciples and the disciples of the Pharisees fast, but your disciples do not fast?" Jesus said to them, "The wedding-guests cannot fast while the bridegroom is with them, can they? As long as they have the bridegroom with them, they cannot fast. The days will come when the bridegroom is taken away from them, and then they will fast on that day. No one sews a piece of unshrunk cloth on an old cloak; otherwise, the patch pulls away from it, the new from the old, and a worse tear is made. And no one puts new wine into old wineskins; otherwise, the wine will burst the skins, and the wine is lost, and so are the skins; but one puts new wine into fresh wineskins." One sabbath he was going through the cornfields; and as they made their way his disciples began to pluck heads of

grain. The Pharisees said to him, "Look, why are they doing what is not lawful on the sabbath?" And he said to them, "Have you never read what David did when he and his companions were hungry and in need of food? He entered the house of God, when Abiathar was high priest, and ate the bread of the Presence, which it is not lawful for any but the priests to eat, and he gave some to his companions." Then he said to them, "The sabbath was made for humankind, and not humankind for the sabbath; so the Son of Man is lord even of the sabbath."

This text is a great example of what's called a Markan sandwich. This is a literary device Mark used throughout his gospel to emphasize what he considered the major points of Jesus' ministry and message. The way it works is Mark takes two stories that are very similar to each other and sandwiches in between them a third, seemingly unrelated story that functions as the key to understanding and interpreting the other two stories. It follows an A-B-A type of format.

In this text, we have two very similar stories about Jesus and his disciples breaking religious laws. In the first story, Jesus and his disciples are criticized for not fasting, and in the second story, they are criticized for breaking the Sabbath. However, sandwiched in between them we find this strange and seemingly out of place analogy Jesus gives about clothing patches and wineskins. This is a perfect example of how a Markan sandwich works, how the seemingly out of place middle story is elucidated by the two stories surrounding it and vice versa.

In Jesus' time, winemakers would put new wine only into new wine skins because they were supple and elastic and therefore were able to expand as the wine inside fermented and gave off carbon dioxide. If you put new wine into old skins that were brittle and already expanded, they would simply burst and you would lose your wine (a truly horrible sin in my book, as well). The hidden message Jesus is saying here is quite powerful and has far-reaching implications. Remember, the analogy is to be understood in the context of the two surrounding stories about Jesus and his disciples breaking Jewish religious laws. Jesus was saying, "My teaching is this new wine and it cannot be contained in the old wineskins of religious rituals, laws, and traditions but is part of a new category of thinking about God and his ways and what it means to be his people." The new wine skins of Jesus' religion is a kind of mystical religion grounded in love and righteous action rather than tribalism and ritualism.

Use Your Jesus Glasses

Another important lesson regarding skepticism can be found in the way Jesus handled Scripture. In Mark 10:2–9, some religious leaders test Jesus over the issue of divorce. They begin by asking him:

> "Is it lawful for a man to divorce his wife?" He answered them, "What did Moses command you?" They said, "Moses allowed a man to write a certificate of dismissal and to divorce her." But Jesus said to them, "Because of your hardness of heart he wrote this commandment for you. But from the beginning of creation, 'God made them male and female. For this reason a man shall leave his father and mother and be joined to his wife, and the two shall become one flesh.' So they are no longer two, but one flesh. Therefore what God has joined together, let no one separate."

The Pharisees are telling him that Moses allowed them to divorce their wives for any old reason and they quote Deut 24:1–4 where Moses makes this allowance. Jesus responds to them by saying, in essence, "Moses allowed you to do that as a concession because your hearts were hard and you were going to divorce anyway. So he made you give your wife a certificate so that she could remarry and/or be taken care of. However, that passage in Deuteronomy does not reflect the true heart and will of God on the matter."

Jesus then goes on to quote passages from Genesis where it says that God does not want couples to break up for just any old reason. Jesus reveals here that the Deuteronomy passage does not reflect the ideal will of God but instead reflects the unique circumstances of a particular time and place in Israel's history. And Jesus made this point with lots of Old Testament passages, namely in his Sermon on the Mount.

> "You have heard that it was said, 'An eye for an eye and a tooth for a tooth.' But I say to you, Do not resist an evildoer. But if anyone strikes you on the right cheek, turn the other also;" (Matt 5:38-39).

Jesus was constantly redefining, reinterpreting, and sometimes even outright countering Old Testament passages in order to reveal the true heart and will of God. In this way, Jesus functions as a lens for us to view Scripture through. And not just Scripture but God, too. John 1:14 says in reference to Jesus, "the Word [of God] became flesh." The Word of God is not really a book of ink and paper but a living person who functioned as the revelation of God's will and love in action. This understanding has a subtle but powerful effect. God's Word is not a book we can quote and use like lawyers against each other. It is a living breathing person who showed us what it means to be godly. When God's Word goes from being words on a page to a person and that person's character and values, it becomes harder to proof text and justify certain actions.

What would have happened if Christians in the American South during the nineteenth century understood God's Word this way? Just 150 years ago, many Christian slave owners in the American South used Scripture to defend their right to own and abuse other human beings. Jefferson Davis, the President of the Confederacy, said, "Slavery was established by the decree of Almighty God . . . it is sanctioned in the Bible, in both Testaments, from Genesis to Revelation."[4] Consider also what Richard Furman, President of the South Carolina Baptist Convention said in 1821, "The right of holding slaves is clearly established in the Holy Scriptures, both by precept and example."[5]

4. Davis, "Slavery in the Bible," para. 1.
5. Early, *Readings in Baptist History*, 82.

These Christians, and others like them, were obviously not reading the Scriptures through the lens of Jesus Christ, the Word of God. But what about today? There are Christians today who use Scripture to say people in same-sex relationships cannot be Christian or join the church. Woman are to be second-class citizens in the church and in the home. You can find a passage to back up any act of oppression or exclusion you desire. However, if what we believe or think doesn't line up with who Jesus is and what he did and said, then our interpretation of Scripture is wrong. This reveals an important truth—although the Bible is authoritative, our interpretation of it is not always. Our interpretation of Scripture is only authoritative in so much as it lines up with Jesus. You can see how this affects all kinds of issues that relate to faith, politics, ethics, morality, sexuality, gender roles—the list goes on. Jesus is the lens through which we understand what God is saying to us through Scripture.

What Is the Bible?

We need to remember that the Bible is a library, a collection of very different books and literature that spans centuries and was written in multiple languages. In it, we find not only the words of God, but also the words of man. We need to think of the Bible as a very long conversation that has been taking place between humanity and God for thousands of years, and our job is to decipher who is speaking when.

Think of the Bible like this: Imagine if Picasso made a mistake in a painting, and in his frustration, he threw a glass of wine at it thus making the paint run and staining the canvas with wine. Then he took it and threw it in a back room somewhere only to be discovered years later by someone. I suspect that painting would be worth as much or more than any of his others. Not just because it is a Picasso but because it is flawed and reveals an authentic and true side of the artist, the dark side of the artist, his humanity and the painstaking process that is often creativity and inspiration. If you owned that painting, the last thing you would want is someone to come along and clean it up and try to reconstruct what Picasso was trying to paint. That would defeat the point entirely because it would rob the painting of all its meaning and power, its beauty, and its appeal. You would love and honor that painting more for its imperfections than if those imperfections were removed or cleaned up. We should have a similar view of the Bible. When we do, it becomes more alive to us and something more beautiful and meaningful. It becomes less like a book of rules and more like a painting or a series of paintings that tell our story and the story of our ongoing conversation with God.

What Is Sin?

The understanding of Scripture and Christianity I am positing in this chapter has major implications for how we define sin. Sin is no longer about having the wrong religious methods or customs. If that were true then Jesus was guilty of sin for breaking the Sabbath, breaking fasts, and breaking lots of purity laws by touching the sick, eating and drinking with sinners, and conversing with Gentile women.

Jesus radically redefined sin in his day as simply that which is unjust and harms others. When Jesus said that the entirety of Scripture can be summed up in the command to love others as yourself (Matt 7:12), he was not just establishing a religion based on love and empathy rather than right belief and ritual, but he was creating a moral standard based on love and empathy rather than religion. In this way, ironically, the prominent atheist Sam Harris and Jesus agree that morality needs to be measured by asking ourselves, "What is best for human well-being?"[6]

Maximizing human well-being was the heart of Jesus' ministry. He spent all his time feeding the hungry, healing the sick, and denouncing those with wealth and power who take advantage of those without. He makes it clear that to inhibit human well-being

6. Harris, *Moral Landscape*, 3.

is sin as he condemns those who did not feed the hungry, give water to the thirsty, clothe the naked, visit the sick, and welcome the stranger (Matt 25). Therefore, sin can be simply understood as that which unjustly harms another. I say *unjustly* because we all can think of examples where harming someone is justified (e.g., getting fired for underperforming on the job, getting arrested and/ or sentenced for a crime, divorce under certain circumstances, justifiable violence).

Implications for the LGBT Community

This understanding of sin has some real-world consequences for us today, namely surrounding sex and sexuality. With this understanding of sin, we cannot deem a same-sex relationship anymore sinful than an opposite-sex relationship. The only question that matters is, who is being hurt in a same-sex relationship? Fundamentalists would respond and say that the individuals involved may not be getting hurt in an obvious way, but they are certainly being hurt spiritually by damning themselves to hell. More to the point, fundamentalists argue that same-sex relationships are harmful because they undermine the sanctity of marriage and the most basic concepts of decency and morality in our society. Those who buy into this slippery-slope argument claim that legalizing same-sex marriage could lead to the legalization of interspecies marriages between people and their pets and widespread polygamy. Similar kinds of ridiculous and paranoid arguments were made about interracial marriages decades ago. Xenophobia and bigotry, not logic and critical thinking, almost always animate such arguments.

I believe the question—can you be a Christian and be in a same-sex relationship?—is the circumcision question of the day in the church. And just like any circumcision question, it is a nonstarter as previously discussed in this chapter. But this does not mean that anything goes and we should have no standards for sexual behavior. Sexuality, like every other behavior, needs to be measured by the question—what's best for my well-being and the well-being of others? I would argue that when we treat sex as something we just do for fun, we often harm others and ourselves.

A great example of this can be seen in the movie *Trainwreck* with Amy Schumer. The movie is all about the trainwreck of a life she creates for herself by sleeping around and using and abusing people like drugs and alcohol, with which she also has a problem. In the end, she comes to discover that she is really hurting others and herself by living this way and so she changes. Here we see how casual sex objectifies and devalues people and ourselves. Add to that the possibility of unwanted pregnancies and STDs, and much potential for harm exists.

Sexuality is a good object lesson for how we should define sin as Christians. When we enter into the skepticism stage we begin to critique more than just how we read Scripture and understand God but what it means to be religious and moral agents. Understanding sin as that which unjustly harms another or that which inhibits human well-being sets us free from oppressive religious ideologies that ironically *are* sinful. For example, it is unjustly harmful to tell LGBT people that if they don't remain celibate, they are going to hell. It is unjustly harmful to tell them they cannot be Christian unless they remain single. I would argue that that is sinful and abusive. As someone who attends the annual Gay Christian Network conference, I have heard countless stories from LGBT Christians who suffer from depression, suicidal tendencies, and all manner of stress-related maladies because they grew up being told that they are evil and that God thinks they're disgusting. That's harmful. That's sinful.

The Truth Will Set You Free

A common saying in the radical theology movement is, "Those who least understand theory are most enslaved by it."[7] By *theory*, we mean a system of thought, such as theology or philosophy that

7. Rollins, "Why Atheists Need," para. 8.

functions as the lens through which one looks at the world. Those who least understand the theology or philosophy they are working out of are most oppressed by it. We all live out of systems of thought that function as the guidance system for our lives. They are like the operating system on a computer—constantly running in the background in hidden ways, processing and organizing information in ways that influence what we see and hear. The less we understand about our operating system the more we are unknowingly controlled by it.

A great example of this can be seen in a parable about two college professors who were having lunch together one day. One of them was the chair of the physics department, the other was the chair of the philosophy department.

During the meal, the physics professor said to his colleague, "Philosophy is interesting but ultimately irrelevant. What really only matters is the material universe and understanding how nature works. What inventions and technological breakthroughs has philosophy ever given us?"

After giving his question some thought the philosopher replied, "So you think that science is very important, huh?"

"Yes, of course," responded the physicist.

"Why," asked the philosopher.

"Well, because—"

And before he could say anything further, the philosopher said, "Now you're doing philosophy."

The thing about philosophy is that everyone is a philosopher whether they know it or not. Understanding the philosophy you are working out of is key to understanding why you do what you do and why you think what you think. Understanding the philosophy you are working out of reveals the hidden presuppositions and assumptions you hold. For example, when somebody asks, "Is Christianity more about what you believe or what you do?" the hidden presupposition is that a meaningful distinction exists between your beliefs and actions when one does not. Your beliefs are your actions. When we don't understand the hidden presuppositions we are working out of, we are enslaved to them. They control us.

Part of my job as a pastor is to play the part of the skeptic. I do this by revealing the hidden presuppositions the community is working out of so that we can be set free and make informed decisions about how we want to live and think. Knowledge is power and the truth sets us free. That's why philosophy matters and it especially matters to us Christians because theology is actually a kind of philosophy.

One cannot separate philosophy from theology any more than one can separate hydrogen from water and still have water. Theology is a kind of philosophy. It is a way of asking questions about what it means to be human and why we are here and why our lives matter and why anything matters. Why does good and evil matter? Why does love matter? Theology is way of answering these questions in a deeper way, in a way that uses the language of the soul, a poetic language that attempts to do justice to the transcendent aspects of our humanity and our experience of the world. Theology is a kind of mystical philosophy, a philosophy that attempts to respond to the mystical parts of our experience. They are ways that we explore and express what it means to be human—these deep aspects of who we are—which also means that theology and philosophy are something we do.

God doesn't do theology and philosophy; we do. Theology may be inspired by God and the divine, but ultimately, we are the ones constructing religions, beliefs, traditions, and sacred writings in response to God. Theology is always a human construct. By not understanding this and instead by thinking that theology is downloaded from God like software off the Internet, or by thinking it is a kind of black magic that must be maintained or else, this is how we become enslaved and oppressed by it.

This doesn't mean that our sacred texts and traditions are not meaningful or powerful but it alters our understanding of what meaning and power are. Our constructs are meaningful and powerful as stories that inform and form our lives. Just as words have meaning and power, "death and life are in the power of the tongue" (Prov 18:21) so our stories and religious constructs have such power. Perhaps this proverb should read, "death and life are in the power of the construct." Our words, religious beliefs, rituals, and traditions hold powers to shape our lives and world, to give life or to take it.

Engaging the Other

Perhaps the hardest thing about the skepticism stage is learning how to engage with the other whose views and behaviors are very different from our own. Growing up in a fundamentalist tradition taught me to stay away from those with different beliefs and views unless I was being an effective witness. In general, those outside our faith were viewed as threats to be avoided or converted.

When I was twenty-three, I found out that my close friend Alan was gay. I had heard through the grapevine that he was going to certain bars and making out with guys. I called him to see if this was true and he admitted it. I promptly informed him that 1 Cor 5 said that I am not supposed to have anything to do with an "immoral brother" and until he repented, he and I couldn't be friends anymore. Alan said very nonchalantly that he understood, and we said goodbye. The pastor of our church heard about what I did and called to commend me. I felt proud that I had done the right thing despite how hard it was, it also felt good to get a special pat on the back from my pastor. Alan stopped coming to church, and we didn't speak for thirteen years until I reached out to him on Facebook and apologized. He forgave me, but I still wince when I think about how I hurt him.

This kind of thing happens all the time in communities like the one I grew up in. The "other" is to be avoided or converted because their beliefs and behaviors could corrupt an individual and/or the community. This is but one of several ways we tend to engage the other whose beliefs and practices are different from our own. Rollins described them well in an interview:

> I either try and consume you, to make you like me. And if I can't do that I want to vomit you out. I want to get you out from my social body because I can't integrate your difference. Or I might tolerate you as long as you don't tell me what you believe and hide it behind closed doors. Or I

engage in interfaith dialogue when we discuss where we're both in agreement. We [need] to reject all four of those because in all four I'm right. In the first three, I'm right and you're wrong and in the last one we're both right.[8]

These four methods of engagement can be summarized as *consume, vomit, tolerate, agree.* Rollins instead suggests a fifth way that we engage the other that can be summarized as *see.* This is where we learn to see ourselves through the eyes of the other and learn to see how our beliefs and practices are strange to them. By doing so, we learn to see how our beliefs and practices may be wrong or contingent and not some kind of universal timeless truth. However, this takes humility and courage as it opens us up to real change. This approach also builds bridges and creates healthy communities where diversity is truly valued. And this strikes me as very Christ-like as Jesus did not try to convert the other (e.g., the Samaritan, the Roman centurion, the Gentile) to his religion of Judaism but instead embraced their differences.

Conclusion

To be a Christian is to be converted to Jesus' way of living in the world, which means to be converted to loving the other, the one who is considered an outcast for religious, social, or political reasons. But it also means to be converted to constant conversion, constant skepticism, and deconstruction of our beliefs so that we might find God where he really is—not locked away in the old wine skins of our religious traditions and beliefs, but out here in the midst of life as it actually is with all of its sufferings and joys, successes, and failures.

The fact is, many people come to faith because their lives are in chaos and disorder and they are looking for some kind of structure that promises order, certainty, and fulfillment. When the church becomes the structure that promises these things, it becomes oppressive and functions like a drug, something that we

8. Rollins, "Courageous Conversations," 2:47–3:17.

use to cover up our brokenness and suffering.[9] This is what fundamentalism does and many within it eventually react against it with questions and doubts only to find themselves ostracized and traumatized by the very structure that they thought would save them. However, what Christ calls us into and what the good news is all about is a new way of being in the world where we experience God not so much in a religious system but as that which permeates every aspect of life and being itself. This is what it means to be a mystic, and I would argue what Christianity is all about.

9. Rollins, *Idolatry of God,* 23.

5

Mysticism

The religions start from mysticism. There is no other way
to start a religion. But, I compare this to a volcano that
gushes forth . . . and then . . . the magma flows down the
sides of the mountain and cools off. And when it reaches
the bottom, it's just rocks. You'd never guess that there
was fire in it. So after a couple of hundred years, or two
thousand years or more, what was once alive is dead
rock. Doctrine becomes doctrinaire. Morals become
moralistic. Ritual becomes ritualistic. What do we do
with it? We have to push through this crust and go to the
fire that's within it.[1] —David Steindl-Rast

WHILE PECK'S MODEL HAS mysticism as the last stage in our spiritual journey and I have it here toward the end of this book, the fact
is it is everywhere in between. We find ourselves traversing the
various stages of our spiritual journeys because we sense a call by
something we know not what. Something tugs on our hearts and
calls us to look deeper into our religious artifacts for the animating
force behind them, for the fire within them as Rast puts it.

---

1. Steindl-Rast, "Monk and the Rabbi," 6:50–7:43.

This fire is called a lot of things. Rast and Peck described it as mysticism. John Caputo described it as the "event" or the "unconditional." To be sure, it is a fire and it burns in the heart of humanity regardless of ethnicity, culture, time, and space. This is why we find religion everywhere from the grand cathedrals of Europe to the tiny shaman hut in the remotest jungle on Earth. This is why we find proto-religious rituals being practiced perhaps more than a hundred thousand years ago by our pre-human ancestors.[2] Religion is everywhere because the fire is everywhere.

The simplest way to describe this fire is to say it is like a sixth sense. It is this inescapable notion that life is meaningful and that things like love and beauty are meaningful. It is a sense of transcendence that goes beyond what we can define or describe. It's not so much something we have, but something that has us.[3] Perhaps life is meaningless and we are just an anomaly of nature. Perhaps there is no God or afterlife, but that doesn't mean that love and meaning don't exist. Love creates meaning in the same way that light naturally produces heat. You cannot have one without the other. Even an atheist who is convinced that life and existence is meaningless cannot help but find life meaningful when they love something or someone. As Rollins put it:

> When someone is in love he cannot help but experience the world as meaningful, even if he doesn't believe it is. While the one who does not love cannot help but experience the world as meaningless, even if he believes that the world is meaningful. Love then infuses the world with meaning regardless of what one believes about it.[4]

Thus, the fire burns even in the hearts of those who claim there is no fire. Religion is what we construct in response to the fire. Ritual and belief is a language of the soul, a vocabulary we create for the ineffable and transcendent aspects of our experience. This means there is nothing magical about our vocabularies.

2. Lieberman, *Uniquely Human*, 163.

3. Caputo, *Folly of God*, 29.

4. Rollins, *Idolatry of God*, 139.

Our religions are not the physics and chemistry of the supernatural realm. They are not the sciences we learn to heal the sick, get prayers answered, and obtain eternal life. There is nothing magical about communion, baptism, tithing, etc. These things are cultural constructs, and like anything that is constructed, they can be deconstructed and understood as contingent and historical.

The Art of Deconstruction

Deconstruction does not mean *destruction*. Think of deconstruction as a very creative act like the way that someone might take a car's engine apart in order to understand how it works and in the process of reconstructing it, learn how to repair it, how to maintain it, or make it run better. Or think of deconstruction as being like someone who tears down the wall between their kitchen and dining room for the purpose of making the space more open and hospitable for entertaining. Here we see how deconstruction can be a kind of construction, as a new space is created that increases aesthetic beauty, hospitality, and enjoyment.

Deconstruction teaches us that nothing is new under the sun, every construct is a remix, and everything is contingent upon something else, be it language, culture, religion, etc. However, deconstruction also teaches us that religion and theology, while contingent and deconstructable, are responses to something undeconstructable, something ineffable as Caputo puts it:

> The real interest of theology is in something deeper than God, deep within God, and deep within ourselves, something older and deeper than the debates that rage up above about believing and not believing in God, in the existence or non-existence of a Supreme Being.[5]

Theology is not so much about God as it is about what is going on in the name of God, what we mean when we talk about God and construct a vocabulary of words, beliefs, and practices to

5. Caputo, *Folly of God*, 19.

articulate it.[6] Theology is ultimately about the mystical, the fire, the event, the unconditional, the ineffable, and the undeconstructable that lies at the heart of God. It is that which we are constantly reaching toward with our religious beliefs and practices but what always escapes our grasp. If we could grasp it, then it wouldn't be worth all this trouble. But it is worth the trouble because we cannot grasp it. We catch a glimpse of it in a piece of music that moves us, a star-filled night sky that fills us with awe and wonder, or in a selfless act of love and grace. It is what we speak of when we speak of God in the deepest sense of the word. It is the muse of countless philosophers, artists, scientists, and theologians.

Ultimately, we are all believers in the religion of the undeconstructable. We all attend this church and pray to this God whether we know it or not. Whether a real God exists or not is irrelevant in the religion of the undeconstructable. The undeconstructable insists, as Caputo might put it, and that is enough. This is the hidden religion within Christianity and any religion worth its salt. This is what Bonhoeffer was getting at with his talk of "religionless Christianity." By this, he didn't mean a Christianity without religious beliefs and practices, but a Christianity that transcends these things, that sees them as a kind of language of the soul and not undeconstructable artifacts that hold magical powers like Harry Potter's wand.

By deconstructing our traditions like communion and baptism, we discover that they did not originate in Christianity and Jesus did not invent them, but they find their roots in other religions and cultures. Baptism finds its roots not only in Jewish ritual washings that took place at the temple, but also in other ancient Near Eastern and Greco-Roman religions that predate Christianity in which baptism was practiced as a rite of passage or initiation into a cult. Communion finds its roots in both Jewish and pagan sacred meal practices. Speaking in tongues actually finds its roots in the ecstatic speech practices of first-century Greco-Roman religions.[7]

Consider also how the Genesis creation story uses ideas and symbols that are derived from other ancient Near Eastern creation

6. Ibid.

7. Potts, *History of Charisma*, 28-29.

myths like the Enûma Eliš and the Epic of Gilgamesh. In these, we find the same concepts that we find in Genesis of a vast sea pre-existing everything else. The waters beings separated into two realms, Earth and sky. The idea that the gods or a god would cause water to rise up from the Earth to nourish the plants rather than have it rain. The presence of a cunning serpent and plants that offer eternal life. All these things are found in Gen 1–2, but also in other ancient Near Eastern creation myths that predate Genesis.

Why Did Jesus Die?

Just as the ancient writer(s) of Genesis translated concepts from other cultures into their creation myth, so the writers of the New Testament translated Jesus' story into their culture and religious worldview. The Jews were not the first or the only religion in the ancient Near East to come up with the idea of blood sacrifices or atonement rituals to appease a deity. This existed in other religions in the region that predate Judaism.[8] So it shouldn't surprise us that the early church and leaders such as Paul translated Jesus' death into their Jewish context of blood atonement rituals. This means that Jesus didn't die on the cross to appease a blood-thirsty deity or as an act of atoning black magic that would supernaturally erase our sins. There are no metaphysics of redemption, no spiritual due process or certain legal procedures God must abide by to save us from eternal torment.

I must be humble and admit that this is my view on the cross and that I could be wrong. However, if such a God exists I believe we have a moral obligation not to worship him. Such a God would be a sadistic psychopath. Imagine a God that said, "I cannot let you into heaven but must torture you for eternity instead because a proper blood sacrifice was never made for your wrong doings." Worshiping such a being is morally reprehensible and it's in Christianity's best interest to do away with such a deity once and for all.

---

8. Hallo, "Origin of Israelite," para. 1–3.

There is something very human and idolatrous about such atonement theories. Blood sacrifices are not only cruel but idolatrous acts that allow us to believe we can control the uncontrollable, namely God, death, and the afterlife. They are also attempts at controlling others with fear. Who could argue that the fear of a cosmic tyrant who tortures people for having the wrong beliefs has not been a useful tool in the hand of the clergy? How much money and power have they consolidated for themselves by this spiritual coercion over the centuries? It doesn't seem to bother them that nowhere in the Gospels does Jesus give us his atonement theory. Nowhere does he say, "All right, everyone, listen up: I'm going to the cross soon to die for your sins in the tradition of a Hebrew blood-atonement ritual. I'm assuming that most of you know what that is, being Jewish and all . . . For you Gentiles, and for those of you who aren't so sure, study up, because your eternal destiny is contingent upon you understanding this stuff and believing it."

Nowhere does Jesus say anything like this, which of course begs the question, how did Jesus understand his death? Jesus said, "No one has greater love than this, to lay down one's life for one's friends" (John 15:13). This is exactly why Jesus died. He laid down his life for his friends. He died for those he loved, and it's pretty easy to understand how this happened.

For years, Jesus was creating the circumstances that would lead to his arrest and death, but the final straw came when during Passover week, he went into the temple and flipped over the tables of the money changers and drove them out. The temple priests and authorities saw this as the final straw because he was now disrupting not just their religious and social power but their financial power, too. Thus they issued a warrant for his arrest and brought him before Pontius Pilate to make a case that he was inciting social unrest with his teachings.

In the Roman Empire, inciting any kind of social unrest, be it political, religious, or economic, was punishable by death. The Empire maintained control over its regions through a zero-tolerance policy for any kind of social uprising. Jesus wasn't stupid; he knew what he was doing. He predicted his death multiple times throughout the Gospels. He understood the political and religious climate he was living in and that he was on a road to arrest and execution. And yet he continued down that road anyway. Why? The answer is simple: love.

Jesus spoke out and fought against the sinful religious and political powers of his day that oppressed the sick, the poor, women, and those of different ethnic and religious backgrounds such as Samaritans and Gentiles. Jesus stood against them and thereby stood up for the oppressed and downtrodden, and for this, he died.[9] Period. That's it. Because again, no one has greater love than this, to lay down one's life for one's friends.

The Gospel and the cross are primarily about a man dying for his friends, dying because he refused to look the other way while they were being abused and oppressed, especially by the so-called religious elite. In this way, Jesus died for the unjust, selfish, and bigoted ways we treat each other. He who knew no sin took upon himself the sin of us all because we are all this way.

Countless people over the course of world history have died for others and good causes. But Jesus represents more than just another human martyr; he represents the martyrdom of God himself for the cause of justice and the cause of us, and this has so much added meaning. Jesus' death is "a divine 'no' to injustice"; as Caputo put it.[10] Jesus' death is a divine "no" to hypocrisy, selfishness and bigotry. But Jesus' death is also a divine "yes" to the opposite of these things—to life, love, and justice.

When Jesus said, "Take up [your] cross and follow me" (Matt 16:24, Luke 9:23) he was saying, "Love like me. Love no matter what, even if they kill you for it." This is what is so good about the Good News. This is what salvation looks like. This is what resurrection looks like. This is what it looks like to die to the world and live again in Christ. This is what it means that Christ delivered us from the power of sin and death. We find God and life in the simple act of love itself and laying down our lives for each other.

9. Sandlin, "God Did Not Kill," para. 20–24.

10. Caputo, *Weakness of God*, 45.

The cross doesn't represent some kind of black magic that God used to erase our sins or pay a debt to Satan. The cross is a demonstration of love conquering sin. Who could argue that Jesus' love didn't end up conquering the hatred of those who crucified him? Who could argue that Jesus' love hasn't been conquering the world since then? As Caputo said:

> But in the powerlessness of that death, the word of God rose up in majesty as a word of contradiction, as the Spirit of God, as a specter, as a ghostly event that haunts us.[11]

We are haunted by the radical love of Jesus, and like any proper haunting, it spooks us and makes us uncomfortable. Fundamentalism is haunted by this God who dies and shows us there is nothing magical about scapegoats, blood sacrifices, or any religious ritual. Fundamentalism is haunted by the spirit of Jesus' radical love. No exorcism can be performed that cleanses our religious structures from this spirit. Confessional theology/religion is haunted by what is called radical theology, this simultaneously ancient and postmodern movement of deconstruction that elucidates what is really real in our religion.[12]

Radical theology is like Rast's metaphor from the beginning of this chapter. It's a way of finding the fire within the rocks. The fire (mysticism) that gave birth to the rocks (confessional theologies) still resides deep within them, deep within the crust of the Earth. One has only to dig deep enough to find it. Our task as heretics, as Stage IV: Mystics, and as practitioners of radical theology, is to dig down and bring this fire to the surface. In this we find a kind of resurrection, a being born again.

Pyro-theology

When I was in high school, I worked for a forest preserve in my hometown of Glenview, Illinois, a northern suburb of Chicago.

---

11. Ibid., 44.
12. Caputo, *Insistence*, 104.

Most of my job was spent sweeping and mopping floors, but once a year I would be involved in a prairie burn. A part of the preserve that was under our care was a remnant of the old Midwestern prairie that used to stretch from Ohio to Colorado. It was a savannah made up of tall grasses and wild flowers. Every year as a part of our responsibility to maintain it, we would burn part of it down. Such a fire was necessary in order to renew it and keep it healthy. The fire would burn up the dead plants and kill off disease and pests. It would also renew the soil and replenish it with nitrogen and carbon from the burned organics. The next year, the prairie would come back stronger and healthier than before. Such fires happen naturally all the time by lightning strikes and are an integral part of forest and grassland health. In some coniferous forests, fires are actually a key component in the reproduction of trees that depend on the fire's heat to release the seeds in their cones. Here we see how fire can simultaneously be a destructive and life-giving force.

The same principle applies to what Rollins calls, "pyro-theology."[13] Here we find the idea that we must incinerate our idolatrous relationship to faith and religion so that something new and healthy may come to life. In pyro-theology we find the idea that faith is found in the embrace of doubt, peace in the embrace of suffering, and life in the embrace of death. This is the heart of what I am talking about in this book and the perverse heart of Christianity itself. We undergo a crucifixion to experience a resurrection. We must embrace Stage I: Chaos to arrive at Stage IV: Mysticism. We must not numb ourselves to the truth of our lives with the drug of Stage II: Fundamentalism. But if we do, we must deconstruct it with Stage III: Skepticism and learn once and for all to embrace the chaos and truth.

Pyro-theology does not only teach us to deconstruct our texts and traditions but to acknowledge our doubt and unknowing. We do this not to destroy our faith but so that in the process we might find a deeper faith—a faith beyond belief, if you will.[14] This is faith understood as a way of living in the world rather than

13. Rollins, *Insurrection*, 173.
14. Rollins, "Questioning Theology," para. 6.

as a set of emotive beliefs. Although this may seem like the death of faith and spirituality at first, like a forest fire, it is actually the means by which faith and spirituality survive and thrive.

Think of pyro-theology as being not unlike Alcoholics Anonymous. When you first attend AA, you have to introduce yourself and acknowledge your addiction by saying, "Hi, my name is Aaron, and I am an addict." In response, people welcome you and it's in this environment of radical honesty, shared suffering, and nonjudgmentalism that people find sobriety and healing.[15] This is the way the church should be. It should be a place where we acknowledge our deepest fears, doubts, and brokenness and thereby rob these things of their sting. It should be a place where we share in each other's sufferings and thereby find healing. It should be a place where we learn to be okay not being okay. But this is really challenging. It means giving up our fundamentalism and any guarantee that God is going to save the day, which is the deepest meaning of sharing in Christ's crucifixion.

The Perverse Core of Christianity

At the cross, Jesus cried out, "My God, my God why have you forsaken me?" (Matt 27:46). Here, we find God despairing, alone, and suffering in the world, God powerless and weak in the world. In order to clean up this problematic text, the church has sought to explain it away by telling us that Jesus didn't really mean what he said. The God side of Jesus knew everything was okay all along—only the human side was really suffering. The God side of Jesus still believed God was in control but he had to say this in order to fool Satan or the Romans, we are told. But to believe that is to completely rob what Jesus said and experienced of any real depth—it is to rob the cross of any real meaning. It turns the cross into a puppet theatre and a really sick and twisted kind of puppet theatre, at that.

But the problem is, we are willing to believe such things in order to protect ourselves from the horror of the cross, from the terrifying

---

15. Rollins, *Divine Magician*, 46.

idea that Jesus doubted and despaired. We want to protect ourselves from that so that we don't have to acknowledge our own doubt and despair because that's painful and scary. And so we come to church and engage in religious beliefs and practices to escape these things. We come to church to escape the horror of the cross. And yet Jesus calls us to embrace it when he said, "If any want to become my followers, let them deny themselves and take up their cross and follow me" (Matt 16:24). The place we are following Jesus to is that place where we too will cry out, "My God, my God why have you forsaken me?" That place where we too will acknowledge the absence of God in the world and undergo a kind of death. This is the perverse core of Christianity. This is what Paul meant when he said:

> We proclaim Christ crucified, a stumbling block to Jews and foolishness to Gentiles, but to those who are the called, [it is] the power of God and the wisdom of God (1 Cor 1:23–24).

This idea that God is weak and powerless in the world and is killed by mere mortals is foolishness, shocking, and offensive. But what we see as offensive, weak, and foolish, God sees as wisdom and strength. This means that before we can begin to take seriously and understand the resurrection of God in the world, we must first take seriously and understand his death because I think we experience both, and I think as Christians we are called to bear witness to both.

I think a tendency exists among the various church traditions to either focus more on the cross or the resurrection as though they are mutually exclusive events when in fact they are like two sides of the same coin as they are of equal importance. Arguing over whether Christianity is more about the cross or the resurrection is like arguing over whether a car engine is more about the pistons or the cylinders. The question is a nonstarter because it is based on a false assumption about the relationship between things. Therefore, as Christians we must affirm the cross and the resurrection simultaneously and say, "God is dead, long live God," to put it in the words of Caputo.[16]

---

16. Caputo, *Insistence*, 123.

Some may say that sounds like a paradox. And it is. The kingdom of God is full of paradoxical truths. Jesus said things like, "the last will be first, and the first will be last" (Matt 20:16). "Those who find their life will lose it, and those who lose their life for my sake will find it" (Matt 10:39). This is the strange paradoxical nature of the kingdom of God that Jesus proclaimed. And perhaps the most profound paradoxical truth of the kingdom is this: "God is dead, long live God."

To say this is to speak truthfully about the human condition and our experience in the world while taking hope in our Christianity. But before we can understand what we mean by "long live God," we must first understand what we mean by "God is dead." Before the resurrection comes the crucifixion, before Easter Sunday, Good Friday and Black Saturday. To say God is dead is to say as Bonhoeffer did:

> Christians stand by God in his hour of grieving; that is what distinguished Christians from others. Jesus asked in Gethsemane, "Could you not watch with me one hour?" That is a reversal of what the religious man expects from God. [God needing help?!] Man is summoned to share in God's sufferings at the hands of a godless world.[17]

This was Bonhoeffer's Christianity, and I would argue that it is ours, as well. To say that we are "summoned to share in God's sufferings at the hands of a godless world" means that our faith and religion is about finding oneself in the world as it actually is with all of its sorrows and joys, with all of its beauty and ugliness. To share in God's sufferings means to long for and work for compassion and justice in an uncompassionate and unjust world. This is what it means to keep watch with Christ in Gethsemane, to stay awake with him and pray and weep with him over the world.

This is about taking responsibility in the world, but so often religion is about shirking one's responsibility in the world. For example, in 2005 my wife Emily went down to the Gulf Coast with a group of people from our church in Nashville to help with

---

17. Bethge, *Dietrich Bonhoeffer, Letters and Papers from Prison*, 361.

the Hurricane Katrina cleanup. There were a lot of other church groups and relief organizations down there helping too, but there was this one church that came, set up a tent, and did nothing but stay in that tent all day and pray that God would rebuild people's lives and bring healing to the Gulf Coast. They actually didn't even pray the first two days they were there because their tent hadn't arrived so they sat around, talked, and ate the donated food. All this while everyone else was out there doing the hard work that they were there to pray would get done.

This is a great example of how we can use religion to shirk our responsibilities in the world. I am sure they believed they were doing God's work by spending all day praying in that tent, but the actual work of God was being done by Emily and those others who were picking up the debris and rebuilding people's homes. I would argue that the real praying was being done by these and not by those in the tent. They were being the body of the resurrected Christ, as Paul would say. This is what it looks like to simultaneously embrace the cross and the resurrection and say "God is dead, long live God." It's about taking responsibility in the world as the resurrected body of Christ and not escaping the world. To this, Bonhoeffer wrote:

> The difference between the Christian hope of resurrection and the mythological hope is that the former sends a man back to his life on earth in a wholly new way . . . The Christian has no last line of escape available from earthly tasks and difficulties into the eternal, but, like Christ himself [who said] ("My God, why hast thou forsaken me?"), he must drink the earthly cup to the dregs, and only in his doing so is the crucified and risen Lord with him, and he crucified and risen with Christ.[18]

For Bonhoeffer and for us, Jesus' death represented the death of the religious God, the death of religion as a means of escaping the world and its problems. The death of the ways we use religion to create churches and ideologies that are intolerant and insular.

---

18. Bethge, *Dietrich Bonhoeffer, Letters and Papers from Prison*, 336.

The death of the way we use religion to escape those who have different beliefs and views that might challenge our own.

Dare to Believe

During the time of writing this book, it was around Easter 2016, and I saw a church sign that said "Dare to Believe," which I assume meant "Dare to believe in the resurrection." I agree that is a little daring, but I would argue that it is not daring enough. Let's go further than just believing in the historicity of the resurrection and dare to actually believe that we are the hands and feet of the risen Christ in the world. Let's dare to believe that this is what belief actually looks like. And this is what Jesus teaches us in the parable of the rich man and Lazarus (Luke 16:19–31).

Lazarus was a poor, old beggar who lived just outside a rich man's front gate. He longed to just be given the scraps and leftovers from the rich man's meals but was left to starve to death instead. It came to pass that the rich man died, too, and from his vantage point in hell, he could see Lazarus in heaven sitting with Abraham. The rich man cried out to Abraham and asked him if he would send Lazarus back to Earth to warn his brothers of this fate, so that they might change their ways and avoid hell. Abraham responded by saying that they have the Scriptures and if they don't listen to what God says there, neither will they listen to a man who even comes back from the dead.

Jesus was obviously speaking about his own resurrection in this parable and what it means for the way we live in the world. Keep in mind that Jesus was telling this parable to the Pharisees, and as he was oft to do. Jesus was telling them that they were so closed off to God's will and ways that they would not change even if a resurrected man came to them. I think we Christians often think that if we can just convince people that the resurrection actually took place, they will convert and follow Jesus' teachings. This is why so many Easter sermons focus on trying to prove the resurrection as a historical event.

But Jesus' point here is that a resurrected man means nothing to people whose hearts and minds are already closed to God's will and ways. Jesus' point is that God's will and ways have already been revealed in the Scriptures and more specifically in the presence of the "Lazaruses," all around us. You see, Lazarus represented the presence of God in the rich man's life. Jesus made it quite clear that to care for others, to feed the hungry, to clothe the naked, to give water to the thirsty is to care for him—to love God is to love others (Matt 25:37–40). No meaningful distinction exists. God is found in the real world with real people with all of their brokenness and mess. God is found in the godlessness of the world, the mundane and paltry aspects of everyday life where we least expect him. In other words, God is found in the "Lazaruses," and if we can't find God there, neither will we find him even in some resurrected man.

When we understand this we experience a kind of resurrection, a kind of rebirth, a being born again if you will. This is what it means to say "God is dead, long live God." We find this paradoxical truth embodied so well in the sacrament of baptism. By being immersed in the water, it is symbolic of Jesus' death and going into the ground. By coming back up out of the water, it is symbolic of his resurrection. By partaking in this sacrament, we are saying that we choose to share in God's death and resurrection in the world. We choose to take responsibility as the body of Christ in the world and not deny or ignore the world and its problems or try to explain them away in some theological or religious way. We choose rather to fully enter into the world. This is the meaning of our baptism as a pyro-theological sacrament. I would also argue that this is what it means to believe in the resurrection.

To believe in the resurrection is not about having feelings of certainty about its historicity but about a way of living in the world, as Rollins said:

> I deny the resurrection of Christ every time I do not serve at the feet of the oppressed, each day that I turn my back on the poor; I deny the resurrection of Christ

when I close my ears to the cries of the downtrodden and lend my support to an unjust and corrupt system. However there are moments when I affirm that resurrection, few and far between as they are. I affirm it when I stand up for those who are forced to live on their knees, when I speak for those who have had their tongues torn out, when I cry for those who have no more tears left to shed.[19]

The fact is, we both affirm and deny the resurrection with how we live. Some may say that such a statement is a cop-out, a way of avoiding answering the question directly—do you believe in the resurrection? But the real cop-out is to make faith about emotive belief rather than a way of living in the world. When faith takes the form of things we verbally affirm and believe in our head rather than a way of living, it is a cop-out. Actions don't just speak louder than words—actions are words. How you believe what you believe matters far more than what you believe. I would go further than even that and say, how you believe what you believe *is* what you believe. When we make belief primarily about ideas that we intellectually subscribe to, we not only do not understand belief from a biblical perspective, but our beliefs are actually a kind of unbelief. They become just stories we tell ourselves about ourselves to cover up our doubt and unknowing.[20]

Prayer

Prayer is an important topic to place in this chapter as it needs to be reimagined in the context of Stage IV: Mysticism. To whom exactly are we praying and why? What does it mean to pray in light of our embrace of doubt, mystery, and unknowing? Rollins says, "You have to be a little bit atheist to pray." This is true because to pray is to say that maybe God doesn't know what I need, or maybe God won't act justly and compassionately in the world unless I ask

19. Rollins, "My Confession," para. 4–5.
20. Rollins, *Idolatry of God*, 53.

him to. If we are honest, we have to admit it takes a certain amount of doubt and anxiety to pray, a certain amount of questioning and unknowing about the nature of God.

To pray is to enter into the question—if God is all knowing and all powerful, then why do we need to ask him for anything? I used to really struggle with this question, and I used to think I had a really good answer to it. I thought that God wants us to pray because he wants us to take responsibility in the world. He wants us to care enough about others and ourselves to at least pray for them, and he will not often act or intervene until we do so because he wants to teach us an important lesson about responsibility. The only problem with that understanding of prayer is that it turns God into a gangster who is holding a gun to our heads and will pull the trigger unless we ask him not to.[21] Or God will "allow" the trigger to be pulled unless we ask him to stop it. Therefore, the reason horrible things happen to us or people we care about is because we did not pray or pray enough or with enough faith. This is a horrible understanding of God and prayer and unfortunately it's pretty pervasive.

Another problem is how idolatry comes into play. Idolatry means to objectify a deity into something we have to appease or manipulate in order to be blessed. It is extremely based on self-interest and the questions—what's in it for me? What can I get out of this? It's a very utilitarian relationship. This kind of prayer sees God as our genie in a bottle who fulfills all our wishes and dreams. Or it turns him into just another product in the vending machine of life that promises us happiness and fulfillment. God becomes a car or whatever product we think will make us happy and fulfilled. When prayer becomes a way that we manipulate God and turn him into a vending machine, it is no longer prayer but idolatry.

And this is hard to avoid because I think prayer very easily turns into something idolatrous. This of course raises the question—then why pray at all? If an activity in our lives so easily becomes something unhealthy, then why do it at all? But there are a great deal of things in the world we find enriching that also

21. Boyd, *Benefit of the Doubt*, 37.

can become very unhealthy if misused (e.g., sex, entertainment, exercise, drinking). While prayer can definitely be used in an unhealthy way, the positives outweigh the negatives.

Researchers have done studies that reveal prayer actually has an effect on our physical well-being by altering our emotional state.[22] The connection between the emotional and physical state of our bodies has been known to exist for a long time. Evidence exists that people heal quicker as a result of prayer. But we also know through recent discoveries in quantum physics that consciousness actually alters the material world. One way that this is known to happen is called the observer effect whereby the behavior and state of subatomic particles is actually altered by a conscious observer looking at them. Waves become particles with defined locations only when we observe them; until then, they remain in entangled states where they are simultaneously both waves and particles and are in multiple locations at once. It is still a mystery and may always be so as to why consciousness altars reality like this in such a fundamental way, but it does, and I think this leaves room for the efficacy of prayer.

That being said, I think prayer often functions as less of a communication between us and God and more of a communication between us and each other. A great example of this can be seen in a parable Rollins told:

> There once was this little boy who was being tucked into bed by his parents and Grandmother and when it came time for the boy to pray he prayed, "God, please bless my Mommy, Daddy and Grandma, and help us all get a good nights sleep." Then he looked up for a moment and shouted, "And don't forget to get me a new red bicycle for Christmas!" His Mother was shocked and said, "You don't need to shout, God isn't deaf." "I know that," replied the little boy, "But *Grandma* is."[23]

Here we see a hidden truth about prayer that we all must acknowledge. Prayer is often directed more at each other than

22. Newburg and Waldman, *How God,* 6.
23. Rollins, "Prayer," para. 2.

at God. Prayer is way of ministering to each other. It is a way of bringing comfort and healing to each other in inexplicable ways. It is a way of expressing a deeper form of solidarity with each other in the midst of our sufferings. This is powerful and we should not diminish it in any way.

Perhaps the deepest understanding of prayer is to understand that God is praying to us. This is seen in no better way than in the Lord's Prayer (Matt 6:9-13). Jesus' point was not to give us the perfect formulation of words or the perfect things to ask God for when we pray, but rather I think he meant it as a lesson on embodying prayer with our lives. In this, I think he shows us what it really means to pray.

He began, "Our Father in heaven, hallowed be our name. Your kingdom come, Your will be done, on earth as it is in heaven." The way that the kingdom of God comes to Earth or the way that heaven comes to Earth is if we embody its values and virtues, such as love, compassion, and justice, with our lives as Jesus did. He went on, "Give us this day our daily bread." This only happens as we feed and take care of each other as Jesus commanded us to. The hungry are not fed with prayers but with food brought by real people. "And forgive us our debts as we forgive our debtors." Again, forgiveness is primarily about us doing the forgiving, not God. He concludes, "And do not bring us to the time of trial, but deliver us from the evil one." The kinds of trials and temptations he is speaking about in the context of this prayer, are the temptation we have not to forgive each other, not to feed and provide for each other, not to be agents of God's kingdom on Earth, but instead to succumb to the temptation to be selfish and ignore the world and its problems.

The Lord's Prayer is best understood not so much as a prayer to God but as a prayer to us. And while this is a radical shift in how we think about prayer, it is in keeping with the way we find prayer modeled throughout Jesus' life. In him, we find God praying and weeping over the world as a mother would pray and weep over her own children. The Gospels tell us that Jesus wept and prayed over Jerusalem and its inhabitants (Matt 23:37). The Gospels tell us that

Jesus wept and prayed in the Garden of Gethsemane and asked his disciples to stay awake and weep and pray with him (Matt 26:40–41). This is the reverse of what we are taught to expect from God. We have been told that God doesn't need us, he doesn't need our help; after all, he's God. But if that were true then why, as Caputo said, "is he constantly trying to get in touch with us?"[24] Why all the correspondence? Why the hundreds of pages of Scripture where God is calling upon us, making covenants with us, weeping and praying over us? The truth is, God needs us and he needs us to answer his prayers and he needs us to answer each other's prayers. This is what it means to pray. This is the deepest understanding of prayer. This is Christian prayer. To pray is to answer a call to action. To pray is to be the body of Christ and answer each other's prayers—to embody prayer with our lives as Jesus did.

Conclusion

In John 3, Jesus has a conversation with Nicodemus, a rabbi and Pharisee who is totally confused about Jesus' teachings on needing to be born of the Spirit. Nicodemus actually thought that when Jesus said you must be born again that he meant you must be *physically* born again from your mother somehow, a bizarre thought indeed. But this reveals just how much Jesus was challenging his core understandings of God and spirituality. He could not wrap his mind around what Jesus was saying, and so Jesus in an attempt to clarify, said to him:

> "Do not be astonished that I said to you, 'You must be born from above.' The wind blows where it chooses, and you hear the sound of it, but you do not know where it comes from or where it goes. So it is with everyone who is born of the Spirit." Nicodemus said to him, "How can these things be?" Jesus answered him, "Are you a teacher of Israel, and yet you do not understand these things?" (John 3:7–10).

24. Caputo, *Insistence*, 37.

In other words, Jesus is saying, "What I'm talking about, Nicodemus, will not fit in your current categories of thought." To be born of the Spirit means to born of something like the wind, a mysterious unseen force that is found everywhere and yet you have no idea where it comes from or where it is going next. Remember, Jesus is addressing Nicodemus here, a rabbi and a Pharisee, a member of the Jewish religious establishment. Jesus is trying to get him to think entirely non-religiously. It is as if Jesus is saying to him, "Look, Nicodemus, you are thinking of God only in the terms of your particular religious traditions but I'm talking about thinking of God in much bigger ways."

Jesus is being totally mystical here in how he uses the metaphor of wind to describe the Spirit. To be born of this Spirit means to be born of something fluid and intangible and yet ubiquitous and powerful. Jesus is obviously describing the same Spirit that animated him, which was all about love. To be born of the Spirit therefore simply means to be born of Christ's love and to find God's presence and Spirit in the very act of love itself, which can happen anywhere at any time to anyone. What is more mystical than that?

God is no longer just this object or person that we love but is found and experienced more in the ways we love each other. God is loved not so much in our worship songs and prayers but in the way that love each other. God is experienced more in the act of loving and living than in any religious act or belief. This is mysticism. This is what it means to be born of the Spirit.

But to be born of the Spirit means to undergo a kind of crucifixion first. The death of religion. The death of the religious God. The death of thinking of faith as a matter of right belief instead of right action. This is part of what it means to share in Christ's crucifixion.

The Gospels tell us that upon Jesus' death, the temple curtain was torn in two from top to bottom. This was the curtain that supposedly separated the presence of God from the rest of the world. The meaning is that God's Spirit now dwells everywhere in the world at once and is not confined to some temple or religious system. Or perhaps the meaning is that God's Spirit never was confined there in the first place. Here we see how the death of religion and that of the religious God reveals that all of life is sacred and holy. God, in the deepest and most meaningful sense of the term, is found in simple act of love itself and in life itself with all of its sufferings and joys. God is not found primarily in our religious structures and ideologies but out in the world where life is lived. This idea of finding life through the death of religion is reflected in Peck's model. In order to get to Stage IV: Mysticism, one must die to Stage II: Fundamentalism. In order to be born of the Spirit, Nicodemus had to die to his fundamentalism. He had to put to death his idols of religion and embrace God in the simple act of love itself and as that which permeates every aspect of life.

6

The Church Will (Not) Survive

I THINK IT'S HELPFUL to think about religion as being like a car that can be built to run on either dirty energy or clean energy. Religion that runs on dirty energy, like a car that runs on gasoline, produces emissions that damage the environment and people's health. In a similar way, a religion that runs on the fossil fuels of tribalism, fear, and anxiety pollutes the world with damaging emissions like violence and ignorance. I would argue that much of religion, including the Judaism of Jesus' day and much of Christianity today and throughout history, has run on the fossil fuels of tribalism, fear, and anxiety. Tribalism, meaning this kind of us-versus-them mentality, this need to feel like we are right and others are wrong. Fear and anxiety, meaning our fear of death and meaninglessness and our fear of uncertainty and dissatisfaction. These fossil fuels have been attractive and useful because they are readily available in the human condition. Like oil and natural gas, they are just underneath the surface so to speak, easily accessible, and quite powerful in their ability to control and manipulate people.

However, the byproduct of running the church on these fossil fuels is a world polluted with violence and ignorance. Religion has demonstrated time and time again its unique ability to pollute the world with these things as religious people are too often willing to oppress, marginalize, and even kill others for the crime of heresy and to enforce intellectual embargos on science and those with different views.

The questions are—can we survive on alternative fuels? Can we survive on clean energy? And by clean energy, I mean values such as inclusivity, empathy, humility, and intellectual honesty. Can we survive on the clean energy of "spirit and truth," to use the terminology from the story of Jesus and the Samaritan woman at the well:

> A Samaritan woman came to draw water, and Jesus said to her, "Give me a drink." (His disciples had gone to the city to buy food.) The Samaritan woman said to him, "How is it that you, a Jew, ask a drink of me, a woman of Samaria?" (Jews do not share things in common with Samaritans.) Jesus answered her, "If you knew the gift of God, and who it is that is saying to you, 'Give me a drink', you would have asked him, and he would have given you living water" . . . The woman said to him, "Sir, give me this water, so that I may never be thirsty or have to keep coming here to draw water." Jesus said to her, "Go, call your husband, and come back." The woman answered him, "I have no husband." Jesus said to her, "You are right in saying, 'I have no husband'; for you have had five husbands, and the one you have now is not your husband. What you have said is true!" The woman said to him, "Sir, I see that you are a prophet. Our ancestors worshiped on this mountain, but you say that the place where people must worship is in Jerusalem." Jesus said to her, "Woman, believe me, the hour is coming when you will worship the Father neither on this mountain nor in Jerusalem. You worship what you do not know; we worship what we know, for salvation is from the Jews. But the hour is coming, and is now here, when the true worshipers will worship the Father in spirit and truth, for the Father seeks such as these to worship him. God is spirit, and those who worship him must worship in spirit and truth" (John 4:7–10, 15–24).

So much going is on in this story that deconstructs the religions of both Judaism and Samaritanism and thereby deconstructs religion in general. Jesus and this woman are violating purity laws within each of their religions, as Jews and Samaritans were not supposed to speak to each other and certainly not unrelated men and women. However, the scandal of this scene runs deeper than that as this is a replaying of Jacob and Rebecca's betrothal from Gen 29:1–14.

In the story, Jacob met Rachel at this very same well that Jesus was at with this Samaritan woman. Jacob spoke with Rachel and kissed her and she ran home to tell her family about the man she just met, and the family went out to the well to meet him. The exact same scene unfolded in John 4 with the exception of Jesus kissing this woman. But nevertheless, this intimate moment unfolded between them where Jesus divulged all this personal information he knew about her like the fact that she had been married five times. She was so taken with Jesus that, like Rachel, she ran home to tell her family about the man who as she said, "Knows everything about me." The family followed her back to the well just like Rachel's family did.

The meaning here is powerful. Jesus and this Samaritan woman weren't literally betrothed like Jacob and Rachel were, but they were connected now in a very spiritually intimate way. The subversive and scandalous nature of this text is what's noteworthy. Jesus, as a Jewish man, took this ethnically and spiritually shamed woman and showed her that she was loved and included in God's kingdom. As a result, she became a minister of the Gospel and went and told everyone she knew about Jesus and how he loved her and accepted her for who she was, a five-time married religious heretic. The text tells us that because of her, many Samaritans came to believe. She is actually revered in the Eastern Orthodox Church even today as equal to the other apostles.

It's important to point out that neither this woman nor anyone she led to believe in Jesus' teachings converted to Judaism or stopped being Samaritans. We are left to assume they continued practicing Samaritanism and going to worship at their temple on Mount Gerizim. It is interesting that Jesus didn't convert her or anyone to a particular religion. He had no name for his movement.

The bottom line is, Christianity began not so much as a religion but a critique of religion. It was a deconstruction of religion like Judaism and Samaritanism and an attempt to find the hidden religion within those religions, this religion of spirit and truth that transcended tribal boundaries.

I would argue that this religion of spirit and truth is what Christianity is, and I think it is systemically different from any other understanding of religion in the same way that an electric car is systemically different from a gasoline burning one. It is a religion that runs on the clean energies of empathy, inclusivity, and intellectual honesty.

Can We Survive on Clean Energy?

Like solar power or hydroelectric power, spiritual clean energies do not pollute the world with dangerous emissions. Rather the opposite, one could say that these energies break down the pollutants of violence and ignorance and promote healing and peace. However, the problem with clean energy is the question of its practicality. Can you survive on it? Can you not just survive, but also thrive and flourish on it?

Pertaining to the church, this question means, can the church survive as an institution if it no longer depends on tribalism, fear, and anxiety as incentives to believe or to participate in the religious structure? Can the church survive if it no longer depends on selling snake oil and promising people divine assistance and heavenly rewards for jumping through the right hoops? Can the church survive if we are honest about the Bible and admit that it is not perfect and has texts in it that promote cruelty and bigotry? Can the church survive if people are told there is no literal hell and cosmic torturer to fear? Can the church survive if people are told that Christianity does not have a monopoly on God or the truth? What happens to organized Christianity or any organized religion when you deconstruct it that much and you begin to run it on clean energy/spirit and truth? Does it disappear? Does it cease to exist?

This is a question that has really perplexed me and other like-minded clergy from a variety of traditions. In 2016, I participated in a panel discussion at the University of Southern California about the relevancy of religion in America. The panel consisted of me, a rabbi, a Hindu leader, and another Christian minister. Some of the main questions were, "Is organized religion disappearing in the U.S. as it virtually has already in Western Europe? Is it being replaced by other forms of spirituality?" The answer we agreed upon is yes and no.

It's so common to hear people say today, "I'm spiritual but not religious," which if you think about it, is a very religious thing to say. To say, "I'm spiritual but not religious," is to recognize that religion can take a variety of different forms like volunteering and acts of service, spending time with friends and family, yoga, working out, and enjoying nature. These things can be religious if one practices them to find this sense of peace, depth and transcendence, a sense of connection to something bigger than ourselves. So religion isn't going anywhere when you look at it that way. Consider what Caputo said:

> Every time someone announces the death of God something funny happens on the way to the funeral.[1]

In other words, as soon as one God dies, another one is resurrected to take its place and this is because we as human beings are intrinsically religious creatures. It is our nature to look for the spiritual and the transcendent and find it in a variety of things. So religion is here to stay and rightfully so. However, I think organized religion will continue to lose ground especially as long as it continues to run on the dirty energies of tribalism, fear, and anxiety. An increasing amount of people are being turned off by that today. But ironically, those dirty energies are actually what will ensure that a remnant of organized religion will always be around. It will always exist to some degree for the same reason drug addiction will always

---

1. Caputo, *Folly of God*, 47.

exist to some degree. There will always be those who will want to use religion like a drug to escape from reality and the problems of the world and to cover up their doubt and unknowing. That's a very negative reason why organized religion will always exist, but I think there are some positive reasons, too.

One positive reason, and one that was previously discussed, is that organized religion functions like a language of the soul for us in a similar way that art and literature do. Religion is a beautiful way we express the ineffable and these deep, transcendent parts of who we are that we don't really have a vocabulary for. To lose that would be to lose some enormous part of our humanity. I think for this reason people will always wish to gather regularly to participate in some kind of spiritual community and to practice things such as communion and baptism, singing, praying, reading the Scriptures, and hearing a sermon.

I think these things have lasted as long as they have because they are healthy and connect us with parts of ourselves, each other, and the divine in ways that nothing else can. I also think that organized religions are uniquely effective at organizing people around common values and mobilizing them to make a positive difference in the world. I think that is why so many charities, hospitals, and schools exist that were started by churches. So organized religion is *not* going extinct, but it will continue to lose adherents and change and that's not necessarily a bad thing. I think some changing and downsizing can actually be good for the church even though it is painful.

Switching from fossil fuels to clean energy is always difficult but the end result is that we will stop polluting the world with dangerous emissions. With regards to the church, we will stop polluting the world with violence and ignorance. But again, making the switch is hard and thereby not an attractive option to a lot of people and thereby not a recipe for building a big church. Most people who attend church don't do so to have their beliefs deconstructed and challenged but to have them reinforced. Making the switch to clean energy (i.e., empathy, humility, and intellectual honesty) can be really hard as it means changing the way one uses religion and thinks of religion.

How not to Build a Church

A few years ago I had a conversation with a conservative Christian man who didn't go to my church but who found out what I was teaching and was very upset. He said, "Wow, you must have a huge church because you're telling people exactly what they want to hear—that they can affirm same-sex relationships, there is no hell, etc."

I responded, "No, the irony is that the opposite is true. I don't have a huge church because I'm telling people what they *don't* want to hear."

People in general (I'm speaking about myself here, too, as a recovering fundamentalist) do not like having their closest held ideas and beliefs challenged and deconstructed. That can be traumatic. As Rollins said, "To believe is human; to doubt, divine." The point is, we as human beings all want to believe in things that tell us we have the answers, we are right and those people over there are wrong. It is very human to want to believe in things that give us that sense of certainty and satisfaction, security and power. And the thing is, everybody is offering us this. Pastors, Mercedes Benz, and Anheuser Busch are all telling us to just believe this, think that, buy this car, drink this beer, marry this person, and everything is going to be okay. You will be happy, fulfilled, and life will be great. That is what we really want to hear and everybody is willing to tell us that so that we buy their product or join their church.

What is hard is to hear and believe the opposite, things like: You don't know the answers. You are broken and immersed in unknowing and are full of doubts. Nothing and no one is going to perfectly fulfill you. The Bible is not perfect. You don't know if God exists or if the resurrection actually happened. Christianity is not some kind of black magic that guarantees you heaven if you just jump through all the right hoops.

In general, this is not what we want to hear because we want certainty and satisfaction and therefore this is not a recipe for building a mega church. But there is an increasing number of people coming out of conservative traditions and longing to get sober from the drug of religion. For them, this message is life and peace. Therefore, we can survive and thrive on clean energy and my church, Central Avenue Church, is a great example of this.

Central Avenue Church's Story

I took the lead pastor job at Central right after I graduated from Fuller Seminary in 2009. At this time it wasn't called Central Avenue Church, but First Southern Baptist Church of Glendale (which might as well have been, Stay Away from Here Church of Glendale). It was an old, dying church that had seen its day come and go. There were about twenty-five people left and the average age was probably late sixties. The church was stuck in a time warp. It was built in 1959 and hadn't changed much aesthetically, philosophically, or theologically in fifty years. The faithful remnant saw the writing on the wall and hired me because I was not Southern Baptist and had a background working in church plants. They wanted the church to survive and they knew that meant changing. Some were more comfortable with change than others, but the majority was with me. I was hired to come in and change virtually everything: the name, vision, worship style, aesthetics, and so forth.

I took the job because I saw the possibilities of revitalizing a dying church and making it into something relevant and vibrant. While I wasn't sure exactly how to do that or what that meant, I was confident I could do it with the right people. It's important to understand that I was burnt out by church at this point in my life. Although I loved seminary, the church had become something I had significant misgivings about, not just because of my fundamentalist upbringing but because of my first full-time job in ministry.

Just after getting my BA in Biblical Studies, I got a full-time job for a church in Nashville as a ministry assistant. The lead pastor was something of a tyrant and from the CEO school of thought. He was hyper pragmatic and fairly emotionally disconnected from others. Though he was an honorable and sincere man, he was performance based and mostly concerned with the ABCs of church ministry (attendance, building, and cash). After working there for two-and-a-half years, Emily and I left Nashville for Los Angeles, not sure we wanted to be in ministry at all anymore. When we first got to Los Angeles, we didn't attend church for a year to give ourselves a break. When I took the job at Central in 2009, I was determined to build a different kind of community, one that was nothing like the church I worked for in Nashville or the ones from my childhood. We got there, but it was harder than I thought it would be.

My first six months at Central, I wore a suit on Sunday mornings, and I preached from an enormous old wooden pulpit. Although this drove me crazy, I tried not making any major changes for the first year so that we could get to know each other and so that trust could be built. That being said, one of the first things I did upon getting the job was take the American flag down off the stage and put it in the attic. I did this not because I hate America but because I am too aware of how the cross has been mixed with the flag and feel that nationalism has no place in Christianity. For six months, nobody noticed that I took the flag down. It wasn't until the fourth of July that someone noticed and all hell broke loose.

That year, the fourth fell on a Sunday and one of the older members of our congregation who had served in World War II, noticed the absence of the flag. He proceeded to walk up to me during the worship set and interrogate me as to the whereabouts of Old Glory. I was standing in the front pew so everyone could see him pointing his finger at me and shouting at me over the music. I initially responded by asking him to follow me to the foyer where we could talk about this. Upon arriving in the foyer, I tried explaining to him my reasoning, but he was having none of it. He told me to resign and I said, "I'm going back into the service and the Gospel will be preached today without the American flag present." He responded, "I won't let this service continue!"

When I walked back into the service I was due up on stage to play the drums as I was still on the worship team at this point. While I was playing the drums and for the rest of the service even during my sermon, I was convinced that he was going to interrupt everything and shout me down. His daughters were present, and they thankfully kept him in check but it was a day I will never forget.

The early days at Central were full of stories like this. Progress was slow and while most of the church was supportive, there were a handful of those who weren't. There were battles fought over changing the name, cutting the ties with the Southern Baptist Convention, selling the hand bells, and getting rid of the sanctuary's horrible old, red, carpet. The church was and still is congregational in polity, which means that the members have ultimate power to hire and fire the pastor and veto any decision. This was no hostile takeover and all the major decisions had to have a majority approval. Nevertheless, change was slow and people got disappointed and left.

At the beginning of my second year, we changed the name to Central Avenue Church and became nondenominational. The assumption from those who hired me was that we would experience significant growth because of this. They assumed that the church would grow like crazy if they hired a young pastor, got a worship band, cut their ties with the Southern Baptists, and changed the name. However, even after making all those changes, we went from averaging thirty on Sundays to averaging forty-five, and we hovered there for a couple years.

The original members got disappointed and angry because of this slow growth. They started criticizing my sermons and the worship music, saying that these must have been the reasons we weren't growing much. I tried explaining to them that this was normal and just what it looks like to do church in a post-Christian/post-church culture like Los Angeles. They were having none of it and most of them left. Within three years of being hired, I lost all but two of my original members. I remember one weekday sitting in the sanctuary by myself crying as I wondered how I would make this work. I felt alone and scared and that I didn't know what I was doing.

I didn't know it at the time, but losing that original crew was the best thing that could have happened. They were a blessing for a while and I am so thankful that they hired me and believed in me initially, but they became cancerous. Some were even lying to me about the church's money and concealing a bank account with $30,000 in it. I assume they wanted to hang onto it as seed money to start over with if they ever got enough support to fire me. In the end, such folks left, and we gained full control over the church and its resources. It was as if my handlers were gone, and I was free to experiment and be myself.

The church during this time of transition and upheaval was gaining new members but nothing like the old guard. The people who were coming were in their twenties and thirties and had a pioneering spirit. They shared my vision for building an intellectually honest community that embraced questions and doubts but that also was focused on justice and inclusion. As a result, we became an affirming and inclusive church for the LGBT community. This is somewhat rare in a nondenominational church such as ours. Most affirming churches are progressive higher church traditions like Episcopal and Methodist.

Central is not a monolithic community and not everyone who attends agrees on this matter or any matter. Our goal is not to get everyone to agree or to believe the same things. We don't have a list of doctrines or beliefs on our website or even in our bylaws. There are no membership classes to take where our theology is taught and new members are told to sign a statement of faith. For this reason, Central is a place of welcome for conservatives and progressives. However, if someone is really conservative, Central is probably going to be too uncomfortable for them.

Our Sunday morning service has gone through some changes over the years but it still resembles the standard model. We have a time of music with a full band. There is Scripture reading, a time of prayer, an offering, and a sermon. However, it's the details of how all that is done that is really different.

First of all, the worship director includes songs every week that talk about embracing doubt and unknowing and the absence of God in our lives. Some of the songs talk about loss and suffering in a way that doesn't try to redeem it or make it all okay. He still chooses songs that affirm God's presence and power but nothing too triumphant.

The offering is never pushed as a kind of divine economy—a quid pro quo deal with God—that if you give this, God will bless you back with that. Nowhere in our songs, sermons, offerings, or prayers do we create economies whereby we try to convince people that if they pray enough, tithe enough, believe enough, come to church enough that God will do X, Y, or Z. This is charlatanism and snake-oil selling, and we refuse to engage in it.

I think the primary way radical theology is expressed is through the sermon. My sermons are always focused on at least one of these themes:

1. Deconstructing religion in order to reveal its deeper hidden truths.

2. Deconstructing misunderstandings of texts and Jesus to reveal their subversive nature.

3. Helping people embrace their doubts and unknowing.

4. Helping people acknowledge their suffering instead of repress it.

5. Helping people find the sacred in the secular, God in the midst of life itself, God in the very acts of love, grace, compassion, and justice.

6. Helping people find meaning, joy, and peace not by turning God into a product that guarantees blessings in this life or the afterlife but by showing them that meaning, joy, and peace can be found in the radical embrace of life itself and of each other.

At the end of each sermon, I have a Q&A where the congregation can ask questions about what I said. During my talk, they can text their questions to the person running the slides and they project them up on the screen at the end. This is a simple thing to practice that tells people that church is not a performance but a time where we have this authentic encounter with each other.

Every Sunday, we also have a time in our service called, Prayers of the People. This is where anyone can come forward and share a prayer request. I adopted this from my experience in a Presbyterian church that used it. My understanding is that it is common in some of the more liturgical church traditions. Though some may see this as a vestige of fundamentalism within our church, some in my congregation see it as the most radical thing we do. It is in this time that people share their greatest sorrows and joys. There is a real sense of meeting people in their brokenness and ministering to them in a deeply meaningful way as a community. This time of prayer over sicknesses, financial troubles, and broken relationships is not treated idolatrously and no guarantees are made of divine intervention. Rather, the prayers themselves are an expression of our deepest hopes and our sense of connection to each other and to something transcendent that we cannot explain.

Conclusion

Talking about prayer is a fitting end to this book, as prayer can be thought of as a metaphor for this entire project. Here in these pages, I am praying for the church and to the church that we might be people of spirit and truth, that we might embrace mystery, doubt, and unknowing, that we might be people who find the extraordinary in the ordinary, that we might be people who can celebrate life in all of its brokenness and fragility, that we might be people who can find the sacred in the secular, that we might be people who find the power and presence of God in the simple ways we love and care for each other. This is what it means to be a mystic and to pray. This is what it means to survive and thrive.

In these pages I have endeavored to provide a coherent vision for what a healthy faith and community can look like. However, make no mistake about it, there's nothing easy about this journey. It is a crucifixion and a confrontation with death and meaninglessness. If this doesn't frighten us then we're not really talking about Christianity.

> Even the disciples of Jesus all fled from their master's cross. Christians who do not have the feeling that they must flee the crucified Christ have probably not yet understood him in a sufficiently radical way.[2]

The crucified Christ is a symbol of God's abandonment, a symbol of despair and total loss. Only those who understand this can understand the resurrection. Only those who are willing to empty themselves and identify with the one who emptied himself of all things, including God, can undergo the kind of rebirth and resurrection described here. This is the perverse core of Christianity but it's ultimately a message hope. Here we find in the strange upside down nature of the kingdom of God—those who give up their life find it, the poor become rich, the suffering find peace, and the one who doubts finds faith. Amen.

2. Moltmann, "Crucified God," 47.

Bibliography

Augustine. *Answer to the Pelagians III: The Works of Saint Augustine.* Translated by Roland J. Teske. Hyde Park: New City, 1999.

———. *The Literal Meaning of Genesis.* Translated by John Hammond Taylor. New York: Newman, 1982.

Bethge, Eberhard, ed. *Dietrich Bonhoeffer, Letters and Papers from Prison.* New York: Touchstone, 1997.

Boyd, Gregory A. *The Benefit of the Doubt: Breaking the Idol of Certainty.* Grand Rapids: Baker, 2013.

Calvin, John. *Institutes of the Christian Religion.* Translated by John Allen. Vol I. Philadelphia: Presbyterian Board of Publication and Sabbath School Work, 1921.

Caputo, John D. *The Folly of God: A Theology of the Unconditional.* Salem: Polebridge, 2016.

———. *The Insistence of God: A Theology of Perhaps.* Bloomington: Indiana University Press, 2013.

———. *Philosophy and Theology.* Nashville: Abingdon, 2006.

———. *The Weakness of God: A Theology of the Event.* Bloomington: Indiana University Press, 2006.

Davis, Jefferson. "Slavery in the Bible." http://www.religioustolerance.org/sla_bibl.htm.

DeLay, Tad. *God Is Unconscious: Psychoanalysis and Theology.* Eugene: Wipf and Stock, 2015.

Early, Joseph. *Readings in Baptist History: Four Centuries of Selected Documents.* Nashville: B&H, 2008.

Hallo, William W. "The Origin of Israelite Sacrifice." http://members.bib-arch.org/publication.asp?PubID=BSBA&Volume=37&Issue=6&ArticleID=8.

Harris, Sam. *The Moral Landscape: How Science can Determine Human Values.* New York: Free, 2010.

Heschel, Abraham J. *God in Search of Man.* New York: Farrar, Straus and Giroux, 1955.

Kuyper, Abraham. *Lectures on Calvinism.* Grand Rapids: Eerdmans, 1931.

Lacan, Jacques. *The Triumph of Religion Preceded by Discourse to the Catholics.* Translated by Bruce Fink. Malden, MA: Polity, 2013.

Lieberman, Philip. *Uniquely Human: The Evolution of Speech, Thought, and Selfless Behavior.* Cambridge: Harvard University Press, 1991.

Lipka, Michael. "Religious 'Nones' Are not only Growing They're Becoming More Secular." http://www.pewresearch.org/fact-tank/2015/11/11/religious-nones-are-not-only-growing-theyre-becoming-more-secular/.

Moltmann, Jürgen. *The Crucified God.* Minneapolis: Fortress, 2015.

Newburg, Andrew, and Mark R. Waldman. *How God Changes Your Brain: Breakthrough Findings from a Leading Neuroscientist.* New York: Ballantine, 2009.

Peck, Morgan S. *The Different Drum.* New York: Touchstone, 1987.

Potts, John. *A History of Charisma.* New York: Palgrave Macmillian, 2009.

Ravenhill, Leonard. *Why Revival Tarries.* Bloomington: Bethany House, 1959.

Rollins, Peter. "Courageous Conversations at Whitworth: Peter Rollins." https://www.youtube.com/watch?v=t7tRd6wVeGw.

———. *The Divine Magician: The Disappearance of Religion and the Discovery of Faith.* New York: Howard, 2015.

———. *How not to Speak of God.* Brewster: Paraclete, 2006.

———. *The Idolatry of God: Breaking Our Addiction to Certainty and Satisfaction.* New York: Howard, 2012.

———. *Insurrection: To Believe Is Human; to Doubt, Divine.* New York: Howard, 2011.

———. "Is Fundamentalism a Problem or a Solution to a Problem: A Debate with Lawrence Krauss." http://peterrollins.net/2013/11/is-fundamentalism-a-problem-or-the-solution-to-a-problem-a-debate-with-lawrence-krauss/.

———. "My Confession: I Deny the Resurrection." http://peterrollins.net/2009/01/my-confession-i-deny-the-resurrection/.

———. "Prayer Works." http://peterrollins.net/2011/10/prayer-works/.

———. "Questioning Theology: Reflections of Decentering Practices." http://peterrollins.net/2014/02/questioning-theology-reflections-of-de-centering-practices/.

———. "Why Atheists Need the Church." http://peterrollins.net/2014/06/why-atheists-need-the-church/.

———. "You Don't Need to Be an Atheist to Be a Christian." http://peterrollins.net/2015/02/you-dont-need-to-be-an-atheist-to-be-a-christian/.

Sandlin, Mark. "God Did not Kill Jesus on the Cross for Our Sins." http://www.patheos.com/blogs/thegodarticle/2015/03/god-did-not-kill-jesus-on-the-cross-for-our-sins/.

Satlow, Michael L. "Jewish Constructions of Nakedness in Late Antiquity," *JBL* 116 no. 3 (Autumn, 1997) 431–432.

Steindl-Rast, David. "The Monk and the Rabbi: Mysticism and the Peak Experience." https://www.youtube.com/watch?v=4egjKZe4wJs.

BIBLIOGRAPHY

Tillich, P. *The Protestant Era*. Religion Online, 2003. http://media.sabda.org/
alkitab-2/Religion-Online.org%20Books/Tillich,%20Paul%20-%20
The%20Protestant%20Era.pdf.

Warren, Rick. "10 Spiritual Questions and Their Answers." http://
powertochange.com/discover/faith/tenquestions/.

Žižek, Slavoj. *How to Read Lacan*. New York: Norton, 2006.

Made in the USA
Lexington, KY
03 December 2016